THE FEMALE AMERICAN

THE FEMALE AMERICAN;

OR, THE ADVENTURES OF UNCA ELIZA WINKFIELD

Anonymous (Unca Eliza Winkfield, pseud.)

edited by Michelle Burnham

broadview literary texts

Canadian Cataloguing in Publication Data

Winkfield, Unca Eliza
   The female American, or, The adventures of Unca Eliza Winkfield

(Broadview literary texts)
Includes bibliographical references.
ISBN 1-55111-248-5

I. Burnham, Michelle II. Title. III. Title: Adventures of Unca Eliza Winkfield. IV. Series
ps875.w74f45 2000   813'.1   c00-931066-5

Broadview Press Ltd., is an independent, international publishing house, incorporated in 1985.

North America:
P.O. Box 1243, Peterborough, Ontario, Canada k9j 7h5
3576 California Road, Orchard Park, NY 14127
Tel: (705) 743-8990; Fax: (705) 743-8353
E-mail: customerservice@broadviewpress.com

United Kingdom:
Turpin Distribution Services Ltd.,
Blackhorse Rd, Letchworth, Hertfordshire sg6 1hn
Tel: (1462) 672555; Fax: (1462) 480947
E-mail: turpin@rsc.org

Australia:
St. Clair Press, P.O. Box 287, Rozelle, NSW 2039
Tel: (02) 818-1942; Fax: (02) 418-1923

www.broadviewpress.com

Broadview Press is grateful to Professor Leonard Conolly for editorial advice on this volume.

Broadview Press gratefully acknowledges the financial support of the Book Publishing Industry Development Program, Ministry of Canadian Heritage, Government of Canada.

Text design and composition by George Kirkpatrick

PRINTED IN CANADA

Contents

Acknowledgements

I would like to thank Santa Clara University for a Thomas Terry Research Grant that enabled me to conduct research necessary to the preparation of this edition. I thank also the staffs at the Beinecke Library at Yale University and the Library of Congress for their assistance in locating and reproducing the photographs included in this edition. I am indebted to Paula Backscheider, whose very generous help was indispensable to me both in the early and later stages of this project. For their assistance, suggestions, and willingness to answer my questions, I also thank Mary Chapman, Judy Dunbar, Mark Kamrath, Jody Pinault, Gordon Sayre, and Laura Stevens. My colleagues in the English Department at Santa Clara University provided me with valuable feedback on the introduction. And Kara Thompson's skillful and timely research and proofreading assistance has been an enormous benefit to me and to this volume. I am grateful to the University of North Carolina Press for permission to reprint selections from the following: *The Complete Works of Captain John Smith, 1580-1631*, edited by Philip L. Barbour, with a foreword by Thad W. Tate. Copyright © 1986 by the University of North Carolina Press. For their support for and assistance with this project, I thank Don LePan and Barbara Conolly at Broadview Press. My greatest thanks go to Chip Hebert for his good humor, support, and encouragement; and to Mara Alice Burnham Cassin, to whose extraordinary adventures yet to come this book is dedicated.

"Unca Eliza Winkfield," engraving from *The Female American, or, the Extraordinary Adventures of Unca Eliza Winkfield*, [1800]. Courtesy of the Beinecke Library, Yale University.

Introduction

The Place of the Text

When *The Female American; or, the Adventures of Unca Eliza Winkfield* was first published in London in 1767, only two very brief reviews of it appeared, neither of which gave the novel much in the way of either attention or praise. The notice that appeared in *The Monthly Review*, for example, succinctly summarized and evaluated the book in less than twenty words: "a sort of second *Robinson Crusoe*; full of wonders, and well calculated to make one sort of readers *stare*" (238). Just what "sort of readers" are being identified here – and whether their ensuing "stare" might be one of horror, disdain, disbelief, or fascination – remains unspecified. Dominant eighteenth-century reading practices suggest, however, that this review is addressed to educators or parents concerned about the effects of novel-reading on that population believed to be especially susceptible to the dangerous fascinations of novels: young women. A similar concern may well have motivated the critic writing for *The Critical Review*, a periodical published by "A Society of Gentlemen," who sarcastically insists that *The Female American* would have fared better had it been published in America instead of in England, since an American audience of "wild Indians" would probably have greeted the book with "the most judicious and sincere applause" and thus have saved this particular reviewer "six hours very disagreeable employment" (217).[1] This review, too, does not explain precisely what made the novel so disagreeable, but it is likely that the critic objected both to the boldness and to the implausibility of the adventures depicted in it.[2]

Unfortunately, modern critics have bestowed almost as little

---

1 Both reviews are reproduced in Appendix C.
2 I have located no reviews of *The Female American* in American periodicals. Essays on novels and novel-reading in late eighteenth-century American periodicals, however, echo English fears about the dangerous effects of novels on young readers especially.

attention, and just as little praise, on this novel as its contemporaries did. The only critical account devoted solely to *The Female American* appeared in the inaugural volume of the journal *American Literature*, which introduces the novel as an example of "the literary poverty of eighteenth-century America" and which concludes by assessing its story as "so preposterous that the book has little intrinsic worth" (McDowell 307, 309). Since this short essay appeared in 1929, *The Female American* has received brief and occasional mention by critics interested in the literary representation of European-Indian contact (see Slotkin) or of America in early English fiction (see Heilman), but has otherwise gone unnoticed by scholars and students of either British or American literature. By too easily dismissing or disregarding the novel, however, critics have overlooked its intertextual complexity, its political and social critique, and its significance as a contribution to the trans-Atlantic origins of the English-language novel.[1] The subsequent neglect of this book has unfortunately removed from view a fascinating, complex, and important text that adds a great deal to our understanding of the cross-articulation of gender, empire, and race in the early Anglo-American novel.

It quickly becomes evident to readers of *The Female American* that the *Monthly Review* critic writing in 1767 made a perceptive literary observation by calling it a "second *Robinson Crusoe*," since it is quite clearly indebted to Daniel Defoe's popular 1719 novel of wanderlust, shipwreck, and adventure. Like Defoe's hero, the protagonist of *The Female American* is cast from a ship during a trans-Atlantic voyage and abandoned on a deserted New World island. In both novels, the central figures endure physical and psychological trials and learn to survive and prosper, first in isolation and later in encounters with the indigenous peoples who visit the island. *The Female American* even seems to borrow a number of quite specific details from *Robinson Crusoe*: both protagonists experience illness soon after their arrival on the island, both survey the island from atop a hill, both are visited by hurricanes and an earthquake, both use

---

1   See Armstrong and Tennenhouse for an argument about the "American origins" of the "English novel."

the goats that roam the island as a source of meat, milk and tal-
low from which to make candles, both ascribe their experiences to providence, and both introduce European technology
and religion to the natives who eventually arrive on the island.

But although it resembles *Robinson Crusoe* in outline and
mimics some of its details, *The Female American* is otherwise a
vastly different kind of story than Defoe's. For one thing, its
central character and narrator is a woman. For another, she is
biracial, multilingual, and boasts a transnational heritage. Unca
Eliza Winkfield – the heroine, narrator, and putative author of
the novel – is the daughter of a Native American princess
(whose father, a kind of Powhatan figure, was Virginia's reigning native King) and an English settler (whose father is identified as an actual historical figure who was the Virginia colony's
first President). Although the heroine's experience of living on
a remote island somewhere in the Atlantic Ocean may be anal-
ogous to Crusoe's, *The Female American* revises the narratives of
capitalist accumulation, colonial conquest, and political imperialism that have been associated with Defoe's book. Winkfield's
story engages instead in fantasies of a feminist utopianism and
cross-racial community, both of which are enabled, however, by
a specifically religious form of imperialism. This text therefore
significantly remodels the Crusoe story in ways that not only
make it an intriguing critique of Defoe's work but an important early Anglo-American novel in its own right.

But *Robinson Crusoe* represents only one text within an
astonishingly diverse and complex network of transcontinental
sources that inform the narrative of *The Female American*. The
novel strategically combines in rich and striking ways historical
and literary antecedents from both colonial America and eighteenth-century England. The text appears equally aware of
early English novels such as Aphra Behn's *Oroonoko*, Defoe's
Crusoe, and his many subsequent imitators, and of Elizabethan
and Jacobean descriptions of Virginia written by travelers such
as Thomas Hariot, John Smith, and George Percy. It incorporates as well details of John Eliot's seventeenth-century
missionary activity among the New England Indians, and
eighteenth-century English interest in Egyptology. The book

offers a rare and unusual depiction of the role of women in the projects of New World colonialism and religious conversion and thus deserves consideration alongside other early modern trans-Atlantic representations of women, race, and empire – including works by Mary Rowlandson, Aphra Behn, Charlotte Lennox, and Susanna Rowson.[1]

Texts like these moreover challenge the traditional identification of the adventure genre with masculinity, male protagonists, and male writers. Such assumptions allow Martin Green, for example, to dismiss German novels about female castaways as "historical exceptions" to the male genre of the Crusoe adventure story, although these exceptions, he admits, "must be of great interest to feminists" (6). Far from an exception, however, a novel like *The Female American* belongs to a vibrant and increasingly recognized genre of female adventure fiction that complicates the traditional dichotomy between male adventure and female domesticity.[2] It furthermore challenges the critical privilege given to those novels that confirm the ideology of separate spheres, which genders the private realm of the home as female and the public domain as male.[3] The heroines of Samuel Richardson's novels *Pamela* (1740) and *Clarissa* (1747-8), for example, are usually identified with immobility, domesticity, and such passive virtues as submission, obedience, and frailty that reflect eighteenth-century social ideals for women (see Brophy). The heroine of *The Female American*, by contrast, represents a radical alternative to dominant novelistic representations of women and to the lives of their readers.

---

1   Rowlandson's text (1682) narrates her captivity among the New England Indians; Behn's *Oroonoko* (1688) is a novel about slavery and colonialism in Surinam; Lennox's *Harriot Stuart* (1751) is a novelistic romance that takes place in both England and North America; and Rowson's novel *Reuben and Rachel* (1798) tells the story of the descendants of European nobility and Native American royalty. All four depict early modern women in cross-cultural and transnational zones of contact. For a fine study of gender and empire in eighteenth-century English literature, see Brown.

2   For studies of female adventure, see Castiglia, Dugaw, and Kolodny.

3   For recent discussions of the separate sphere debate in American literary history, see "No More Separate Spheres!"

Problems of Truth and Virtue

It did not take long after the publication and subsequent translation of *Robinson Crusoe* for imitations of it to appear throughout Europe. Among these imitations are a number of novels that put a woman in the place of Defoe's hero, novels that Jeannine Blackwell calls "female Robinsonades." According to Blackwell, at least 26 female Robinsonades appeared in Germany, Holland, France, England, and America in the eighteenth and nineteenth centuries – a number that is almost certainly an underestimate. Although *The Female American* does not appear on Blackwell's list, it should be included among this group of novels that tell fantastic stories of female shipwreck and island adventuring. But making such a story legitimate reading material for an eighteenth-century audience – for whom the novel was still a relatively new, and morally suspect, genre – posed a significant series of difficulties, and the first reviews of *The Female American* suggest that this particular attempt did not completely succeed in overcoming those difficulties.

In his study of the English novel and its origins, Michael McKeon argues that the novel emerges during a historical period of instability in the interrelated categories of truth and virtue, an instability characterized by a crisis in the ability to determine whether a narrative is telling the truth and whether a person is really virtuous. Novels *represented* such crises in the stories that they told, but they also *performed* such crises for their readers, who were themselves left uncertain about whether the text they read was truth or fiction and its characters virtuous or corrupt. Indeed, in the eighteenth century novels were almost routinely condemned for being both untrue and immoral, and many worried that novel readers, drawn into the fictional and intriguing world of a novelistic narrative, would be led to desire or imitate the kinds of unrealistic and illicit behavior they encountered in books. In an effort to legitimate their work, novelists almost inevitably attested both to the truthfulness and to the ethical usefulness of their books, insisting that their volume provided moral instruction as well as entertainment to readers. When the novel in question told a story, however, about the very improbable adventures of a woman living alone on an island somewhere in the Atlantic Ocean and fending for herself among the goats, hurricanes, and Indians, such claims to truth could prove difficult to sustain. Moreover, a text that recounted the rather remarkable freedoms of a solitary and independent young woman was especially subject to criticism by those who feared that readers, by desiring to repeat the experiences of novelistic heroines, might lose their virtue.

The author of *The Female American* was clearly aware of these potential criticisms and attempted to accommodate them in part by attesting to the authenticity and educational value of the narrative. For example, the novel's "editor" claims, in the opening advertisement, that the narrative is "both pleasing and instructive, not unworthy of the most sensible reader; highly fit to be perused by the youth of both sexes, as a rational, moral entertainment; and, as such, ... will descend to late posterity, when, most of its contemporaries, founded only in fiction, will have been long forgotten" (see page 33 [headed Advertisement] at the beginning of the text of the novel). But the writers of female Robinsonades like this one obviously had to do much more than simply assert that their stories were virtuous and true. They also engaged a range of plot devices, modes of characterization, and narrative details that, by creating a logical and moral rationale for the heroine's exploits, anticipated objections about inauthenticity and immorality.

The heroine Unca Eliza Winkfield is, for example, free of many of the weaknesses or limitations that characterize Robinson Crusoe. Whereas Crusoe is a disobedient son who defies his father, Winkfield is devoted to her father. Crusoe takes to the sea in an act of resistance to his father's pleas that he adopt the secure but unexciting "middle station" of life. Winkfield, on the other hand, crosses the Atlantic precisely out of obedience to and affection for her father, whose wishes she is carrying out when she finds herself marooned. Crusoe consequently interprets his shipwreck as providential punishment for his defiance and independence, whereas Winkfield's abandonment appears as an unprovoked and undeserved fate. Unca Eliza

Winkfield generally also avoids having to engage in tasks that require specifically masculine forms of knowledge or that would otherwise be easily dismissed as impossible. Thus while Crusoe spends years fashioning and fortifying several residences for himself on the island, Winkfield fortuitously finds an immense dwelling already existing on the island, and locates a manuscript left by a hermit that offers her instructions on how to survive there.

In spite of such attempts to attain a kind of plausibility, the narrator also makes clear from the very beginning of the novel that her experiences can only be classified as extraordinary,[1] particularly when they are compared to the rather repetitive and mundane lives of most women. She implies that it is her uniquely non-domestic existence that has made available to her the opportunities for adventure and mobility typically enjoyed only by men, when she notes that "The lives of women being commonly domestick, the occurrences of them are generally pretty nearly of the same kind; whilst those of men, frequently more vagrant, subject them often to experience greater vicissitudes, many times wonderful and strange. Though a woman, it has been my lot to have experienced much of the latter" (35). On the one hand, this remarkable passage aims to minimize the narrative's more illicit and fantastic dimensions by making them more believable: if Unca Eliza Winkfield's adventures seem implausible, it is only because women are not given the opportunity for more mobility and thus more "wonderful and strange" experiences. But this passage, by drawing attention precisely to the transgressive elements in her story, announces its "dangers" even as it minimizes them. This double-voiced strategy, which can be seen to work throughout the novel, at once appeals to and diminishes the unauthorized desires of readers.

---

1 In fact, the word *extraordinary* appears with remarkable frequency in *The Female American*, and the two nineteenth-century American editions of the novel both add the word to its title: *The Female American; or, the Extraordinary Adventures of Unca Eliza Winkfield*.

Winkfield and Crusoe: Further Comparisons

The discussion above suggests that many of the variations on Defoe's narrative in *The Female American* attempt to render the actions of a female protagonist realistically possible, if not believable. But many of these changes constitute differences that also carry a significant cultural and political charge. We have seen, for example, that Crusoe interprets his series of disasters at sea and his eventual shipwreck as providential punishment for his disobedience to his father. Winkfield's seagoing misfortune, on the other hand, is represented as a cruel and unwarranted response to her refusal to consent to an unwanted marriage. She is abandoned on a remote island by the captain of her ship because she refuses to sign a contract that would bind her to marry his son upon their arrival in England. In order to arrive safely in England this heroine would have to submit to patriarchal tyranny and sacrifice her desires. As Blackwell notes, many other female Robinsonades use this plot device of resistance to an unwanted marriage in order to land their heroines on deserted islands where they typically find themselves living in a utopia and practicing sometimes radical forms of independence and power. Like other such texts, then, *The Female American* critiques the helplessness of women within a coercive marriage market, and it goes on to offer a fantastic alternative to typical female roles within dominant culture.

Such differences as these between Crusoe and Winkfield suggest not just an attempt to fashion a heroine who can participate in unlikely adventures without compromising her virtue, but an attempt to fashion a feminist revision of Defoe's earlier tale. And the primary engine that enables this revision is the specifically "American" identity of Unca Eliza Winkfield. Those elements that make Winkfield an American – her Native American cultural upbringing and identity as the daughter of an Indian princess – are those very elements that enable her to engage in activities and to fashion an identity that would be unavailable to an ordinary English heroine. Winkfield's excuse for rejecting a string of marriage offers from a host of interested suitors, for example, is that none of these men are able to shoot a bow and arrow as effectively as she, a skill developed in the context of her mother's Indian culture. Those actions and abilities that seem most unusual or surprising for a female are invariably explained and legitimized by her status as a female *American*, an identity that strategically allows her to indulge in what would otherwise be, for an *English* woman, transgressive acts and adventures.

But although Unca Eliza Winkfield is represented as extraordinary by virtue of her birth, this novel is also the story of her subsequent development into a powerful and influential religious leader. While her bicultural identity sets the stage for her achievement of this end, it is her experience on the island itself that allows her to arrive there. Upon being deposited on the island, Unca Eliza undergoes a series of difficulties and transformations that add up to a kind of rebirth. She is at first so overwhelmed by her abandonment and isolation that she faints, becomes almost paralyzed with fear, and refuses to explore the island because she "was not fond of rambling" (60). An illness brought on by anxiety over her condition reduces her to a state of near-death. She must literally crawl, like an infant, in order to reach water and shelter. After undergoing a kind of inadvertent baptism in the island's river, she recovers her strength by nursing from the dugs of a she-goat. As her health returns and she regains the ability to walk, Winkfield is figuratively reborn on this New World island. But that rebirth also increasingly resembles something more like a resurrection.

Winkfield begins, in the wake of her cure, not only to adopt a much more fearless relationship to the island but to take on the persona of a prophetess. Whereas previously the idea of "wandering alone was terrifying" (60), she now spends days "rambling about the island" (107), exploring it with pleasure. Like a naturalist, she even records descriptions of the flora and fauna she discovers, including one very strange animal whose very physiology allegorizes colonialist relations. She descends into the underground chambers of the extensive temple in which she has been living, and discovers the coffins of Indian priests and virgins, as well as evidence of the sun-worship that is practiced on the island. She adorns herself with the bracelets and jewels worn by the high-priests of this solar religion, and determines to attempt to convert the Indians to Christianity by speaking to them in their tongue from within the hollow idol that they visit the island to worship. In the process of inhabiting this idol, Winkfield becomes "entombed alive" (88) during an earthquake and, in an attempt to emerge from her premature burial, wounds and bloodies the palms of her hands (88). It would seem that Winkfield's earlier reminder to herself to "imitate Jesus" (70) becomes at this point almost literally realized, for following this experience she ultimately takes up a position among the Indians of a female apostle whose gender, racial, and class identity all facilitate their acceptance of her and of her spiritual teachings.

Critics of *Robinson Crusoe* have long been divided over the religious and economic dimensions of Defoe's novel. Ian Watt, following Karl Marx, argued that Crusoe exemplifies economic individualism and represents a capitalist hero whose narrative is organized by profit, exploitation, and accumulation. For Watt, Crusoe's story celebrates capitalist and imperialist agendas: "discover an island that is desert only because it is barren of owners or competitors, and there build your personal Empire with the help of a Man Friday who needs no wages and makes it much easier to support the white man's burden" (87). Other critics, including Maximilian Novak and J. Paul Hunter, have challenged Watt's emphasis on capitalist economics by foregrounding instead the novel's Puritan elements, insisting that it is best understood as a spiritual autobiography in the tradition of Bunyan's *Pilgrim's Progress*, organized by providences and the experience of conversion.[1] More recently, critics have focused on the ways in which Crusoe's story plays out a colonialist fantasy in its attitudes toward race and culture as well as in its religious and economic assumptions (see Hulme and Dharwadker).

The Female American, however, is difficult to read as either a capitalist lesson plan or a spiritual autobiography, largely because its narrative is less concerned with accumulation – of

---

1 See also White for an anti-economic reading of *Crusoe*. Hulme provides an insightful summary of the economic and religious strands of criticism on Defoe's novel (177-79).

either wealth or piety – than it is with the fantasy of female power exercised within and by means of a Christian colonialist utopia. After becoming shipwrecked on the island, Crusoe begins to stockpile economic wealth and spiritual status, and eventually returns to England both rich and converted. As an only child and the niece of a minister who has guided her early religious instruction, Unca Eliza Winkfield is already wealthy and pious when she lands on the island. In both cases, of course, the New World is robbed of its resources: most of the riches that Winkfield inherits from her Indian mother have already been removed from America to England by her father, and these are further supplemented by the additional treasure she discovers in the tombs beneath the island's temple. This treasure certainly enriches those Winkfields back in England to whom she sends it, but it does not enrich Winkfield herself, who unlike Crusoe chooses in the end to relinquish her possessions and her ties to England in order to remain living among the Indians.

Much like Crusoe, Winkfield vacillates between doubt and conviction, and gains respect and influence through her religious instruction to the natives. But instead of undergoing a fundamental spiritual change herself, Winkfield undergoes a change in power gained by proselytizing the spirit to others. In order to retain that power, Winkfield must forsake England and remain on the island, because it is only on the island and among the Indians that her power as a female apostle remains viable. Whereas Robinson Crusoe sustains, throughout his 28 years on the island, an insistent desire to escape, Unca Eliza Winkfield quickly loses any hopes she first entertained of leaving her newfound utopia. The sense of confinement and isolation she endures become in time the very means by which this later Crusoe escapes European limitations on cross-racial exchange and female liberty. For such reasons, it is not surprising that Unca Eliza is uninterested in leaving the island and ultimately chooses to remain there even when a rescue party arrives for her. Like those European women who elected to remain with the Indians who had taken them captive rather than return to their home culture, Unca Eliza Winkfield locates cultural possibilities among the Indians that would be unavailable to her in England.[1] *The Female American* gives an early novelistic account therefore not of an economic man who practices venture capitalism and political colonialism in order to make of a New World island a small England, but of an apostolic woman who practices missionary zeal and religious colonialism to make of a New World island a cross-racial Christian utopia that remains deliberately isolated from Europe. Indeed, the binary opposition between European and Other that underpins *Crusoe* can hardly be so easily maintained in a book whose protagonist's hybrid identity upsets that very opposition.

The novel's representations of colonialism and slavery are, however, ambivalent at best. At times, both English and Indian characters condemn those practices. Unca's clergyman uncle warns his brother William, Unca's father, that "We have no right to invade the country of another" (37), and when William is later taken captive by the natives of the country he has invaded, the Indian king asks, "we know you not, and have never offended you; why then have you taken possession of our lands, ate our fruits, and made our countrymen prisoners? Had you no lands of your own?" (38). Unlike Crusoe, who gains a kind of monarchic power on his island precisely by enslaving the natives, Winkfield pointedly rejects the Indians' offer to become their queen and even speaks out against slavery (although she of course boards the ship with Indian slaves of her own) when she compares her abandoned condition on the island to "those consigned to slavery for life! forced to bear with accumulated evils" and "slaves to a tyrant, and the subjects of unrelenting cruelty!" (70). But although it seems at such moments to critique *Robinson Crusoe*'s account of the enslavement, exploitation, and conquest of America's natives, this text articulates its own forms of imperialist violence.

Even if the narrative pattern of *The Female American* subordinates personal accumulation and geopolitical expansion to personal divestment and geopolitical isolation, Winkfield still

---

1   The two best-known accounts of women adopted into and remaining among Indian tribes are those of Eunice Williams (see Demos) and Mary Jemison (see Seaver). See also studies of female cross-cultural captivity by Burnham and Castiglia.

benefits both economically and spiritually from her island experience just as Crusoe does. And the Indians suffer the loss of both their native resources and their native religion as a result of her arrival. Rather than a mutually beneficial spiritual exchange between Europe and the Americas, the novel depicts the religious conquest of Indian society; Winkfield even goes so far as to order the sun idol destroyed to ensure that the Indians will never be tempted to worship it again. One might also argue that it is the heroine's religious imperialism, much more than the insistence on her virtue and believability, that serves as the novel's most effective alibi against potential criticisms of her vanity and self-indulgence.

The utopian feminist elements of *The Female American* are compromised not just by its Christian imperialism but by its conclusion with a traditional marriage plot that threatens to erase the fantasy of unrestricted female freedom in which the novel otherwise indulges. This conclusion also complicates the novel's formal qualities. In its last chapters, narrative agency slides from the heroine Unca Eliza Winkfield to her cousin and would-be rescuer John Winkfield Jr., who – despite continued resistance from and an explicit lack of interest on the part of the heroine – succeeds in becoming her husband. As this development takes place in the plot, the narrative voice begins to slip inconsistently and unexpectedly between speakers and between the singular and plural first-person (from "I" to "we"), as if its author were no longer sure who is telling the heroine's story. At the same time, the narrative recounted in the final chapter is often being told at second, third, or even fourth remove; for instance, in explaining to her how he discovered her whereabouts, Unca's cousin tells a story he and his father were told by a merchant captain, who is in turn repeating the story told to him by a reformed pirate named Captain Shore, who had earlier encountered the captain of the ship that left Unca Eliza Winkfield on the island. The resulting confusion between speakers, voices, and direct and indirect discourse is, as Blackwell notes, common enough in other female Robinsonades and in early novels and prose fiction generally. But more importantly to our understanding of this particular novel, these narrative confusions reflect the difficulties of representing female voice. Here as elsewhere in the text, the narrative voice of Unca Eliza Winkfield might be seen to speak, quite strategically, through the mouths of others – including the imagined words of her preacher uncle urging her to take on the project of conversion, and of course the mouth of the idol itself through which she speaks to the Indians. This practice of narrative ventriloquism dislocates the voice of the heroine from her body, and makes it seem as if that voice – while clearly identified as hers – is nevertheless issuing from the lips of male figures who are invested with social and religious authority. This strategy enables the heroine to express sentiments and to engage in vocal performances that, if spoken more directly, might be far more open to censure.

Problems of Authorship and Identity

The title page of *The Female American* indicates that its narrative chronicling the "Adventures of Unca Eliza Winkfield" was "Written by Herself," just as the title page of *Robinson Crusoe* and of countless subsequent Robinsonades claimed to be written by their eponymous heroes and heroines. While Unca Eliza Winkfield is clearly a pseudonym, the author who used that pseudonym remains unidentified, as is the case with several other female Robinsonades. Although a number of critics have made the assumption that its author was American, no evidence exists to substantiate that claim, and we do not know whether the author lived in England or in the American colonies. The publication of the novel cannot resolve this question either. While its first printing in London might suggest an English author, it does not exclude an American one. The only reference within the text itself to its publication seems almost deliberately to muddle the question of its national origins, for the narrator notes that "if ever [her account] should be published *in any country*" (105; emphasis added), it would surely inspire later imitations by male writers.

If the author were in fact a colonial American, *The Female American* would undoubtedly be the first American novel, preceding by over two decades any other competitors for that title. Recent attempts to redefine the category of "American literature," however, suggest that it may be unnecessary to engage in such unsupportable speculations. If we follow William Spengemann in defining American literature not by the identity of authors but by the contents, concerns, and language of the texts themselves, then certainly *The Female American* is an American novel, though not the first one (that claim would still go, as Spengemann argues, to Aphra Behn's 1688 novel set in the West Indies, *Oroonoko*).

The only two subsequent editions of *The Female American* were both published in New England, the first circa 1800 in Newburyport, Massachusetts and the second in Vergennes, Vermont in 1814. This later publishing history may shed no further light on the author's identity, but it does shed a great deal of light on the cultural appeal of the novel, for it indicates that *The Female American* continued to find interested readers and even gained some popularity among a specifically postcolonial, early national *American* audience. When the dismissive critic writing for the *Critical Review* in 1767 sarcastically suggested, therefore, that the novel would find a more appreciative audience in America, he was, in a sense, correct – although not in the way he intended.

These difficulties of establishing the author's national identity are just as insolvable, and perhaps even more frustrating, in relation to the question of gender. Here, too, critics have tended to suppose that *The Female American* was written by a woman. In her discussion of the large percentage of pseudonymous or anonymous female Robinsonades whose authors' real names have not been discovered, Jeannine Blackwell notes that it is tempting to assume these texts were written by unknown women authors. But she goes on to note that such conclusions cannot be supported without evidence, particularly since there are female Robinsonades – including Charles Dibdin's *Hannah Hewit; or, The Female Crusoe* (1792) – that were written by men.

But as disappointing or frustrating as this lack of information may be, it is critical to recognize that it is finally not because of who its author may or may not have been that this novel is important. Whether female or male, American or British, the author of *The Female American* articulated for readers on both sides of the Atlantic an often radical vision of race and gender through an account of a biracial heroine who is able to indulge in a kind of "rambling" mobility and "extraordinary" adventure precisely because she is, as the title declares, an American female. As we have seen, the freedom and power that she experiences are largely legitimized by the novel's religious imperialism and its use of strategic narrative devices. But this heroine's exploits are in the end enabled as well by her identity as a "female American." And *The Female American* is, finally, a book about the potentially extraordinary possibilities of being both female and American.

England and America: Further Sources

Although information about the real author of *The Female American* has, thus far, been impossible to come by, the text that author created makes it possible to discover a great deal about the literary and historical sources that he or she may have used to fashion the novel. The heroine Unca Eliza Winkfield, for instance, is the fictional granddaughter of an actual historical figure. The early part of the novel, which recounts the history of the heroine's family and its relationship to America, declares that her grandfather was Edward Maria Winkfield. Edward Maria Wingfield (which was alternately spelled Winkfield) was the first President of the Virginia colony and the author of "A Discourse on Virginia," a tract that describes the first attempts to establish a settlement at Jamestown and that defends Wingfield from the discredit that had been cast on him by John Smith and others.

Although Wingfield's "Discourse" did not appear in print until 1845, various accounts of the establishment of the Virginia colony and of Wingfield's role in it were available much earlier in narratives by George Percy, John Smith, and others. Both Percy's "Discourse on Virginia" and much of Smith's writings, for example, were included in Samuel Purchas's *Hakluytus Posthumous; or Purchas His Pilgrimes* (1625), a massive multi-volume compendium of travel narratives that followed the project begun by Richard Hakluyt in his *Principall Navigations* (1589). *Purchas His Pilgrimes* included not only works by Smith and Percy but also accounts, such as Thomas Hariot's *Brief and True Narrative*, that Smith borrowed from and reproduced in his *Generall History of Virginia*, a text that is best known for a brief anecdote about Pocahontas that has since become Smith's most famous and most mythologized exploit. *The Female American*'s author was certainly familiar with this episode, since the first few chapters of the novel offer an informed retelling and intriguing elaboration of the Pocahontas legend. William Winkfield, the heroine's father and the son of Edward Maria Winkfield,[1] is a figure who is modeled after both John Smith and John Rolfe. Like John Smith, William Winkfield is taken captive in Virginia by Indians, where he is saved from death by the intervention of the Indian princess, Unca Eliza's mother. Like John Rolfe, William Winkfield marries this Indian princess and has a child with her – thereby giving birth to the heroine of *The Female American*.

The narratives by Hariot, Percy, and Smith are also likely sources for the novel's characterization of the Indians who come to visit and worship on the island, since each of these earlier narratives describe the Indians' practice of sun-worship. Just as often, however, the Indians of *The Female American* resemble ancient Egyptians or even the Aztecs rather more than they do the southern Algonquians encountered by Percy and Smith. The depictions of the Indians' ancient temple and idol of the sun, of the embalmed remains of priests and the ashes of virgins, and the hermit's solitary monastic cell, are probably influenced as well by accounts, whether classical or more contemporary, of ancient pagan and Coptic Egypt. Like the early American materials that inform this novel, such tales of ancient Egypt sometimes contained examples of powerful female figures, including goddesses, prophetesses, and women who took vows of absolute solitude and lived alone, like the anchorite hermits of Coptic Egypt, in the desert.

---

1 The real Edward Maria Wingfield never had any children. See Jocelyn R. Wingfield.

Even if the author of *The Female American* was not familiar with the writings of John Eliot, who was called the "Apostle to the Indians," he or she ascribed Eliot's famous achievement of translating the Bible into the Indian language to the heroine Winkfield. Eliot and others also wrote a number of tracts, published for the Society for the Propagation of the Gospel in New England, that were largely made up of question and answer dialogues between English missionaries and the Indians. These dialogues, which provided evidence to English readers of the Indians' interest in and conversion to Christianity, look very much like the exchanges between Winkfield and the Indians whom she instructs.

While the appendices to this edition of *The Female American* make no effort to be exhaustive, they do include selections from among the most relevant of these sources. Although I have distinguished "English" from "American" sources in the appendices, I have deliberately placed those terms in quotation marks to indicate the inevitable overlap between them: the "American" sources are descriptions of colonial Virginia by English travelers to America, and the "English" sources are novelistic depictions by English writers of the Americas and their inhabitants. The "English" sources include Aphra Behn's account of New World natives from her early novel *Oroonoko*; extensive passages from *Robinson Crusoe* and briefer ones from Defoe's *Serious Reflections*, his second Crusoe novel; and a selection from Peter Longueville's *The Hermit*, the first *Crusoe* imitation. The "American" sources include selections from Thomas Hariot's "Brief and True Report" (including an engraving by Theodore de Bry, based on the original watercolors of John White, from Hariot's 1590 edition); passages from George Percy's "Discourse on Virginia"; and longer selections from John Smith's *Generall History*. The appendices also contain the two 1767 reviews of the novel discussed in the first section of this introduction. Finally, the illustration depicting Unca Eliza Winkfield originally appeared as a frontispiece in the Newburyport edition of *The Female American*.

It bears remembering, however, that the sixteenth- and seventeenth-century accounts of America and its Indians — although they have often served as sources for modern anthropologists – represent European perceptions and assumptions. Moreover, those earlier English attitudes toward America were transformed by eighteenth-century reconceptions of the Indians as noble savages. Rousseau may be the writer best known for deploying the trope of the noble savage, but several texts printed in the year or two prior to the publication of *The Female American* are of particular interest because they fashioned models of American identity out of Indian figures, much as this novel does. Two such titles – William Smith's 1765 *Historical Account of the Expedition Against the Ohio Indians*, and Robert Rogers' 1766 play *Ponteach, or the Savages of America* – are notable for their depiction of Indians as heroic exemplars of the specifically American-identified virtues of independence, patriotism, and love of freedom, despite the fact that both texts were far more popular in England than in America (see Slotkin).

Shifting relations between England and its American colonies are also a means of accounting for this novel's representation of the colonization of the Americas. When *The Female American* was first published in 1767, the French and Indian wars in America were in their final phase, and the Stamp Act had just been passed. England's colonial presence in America was, therefore, far more complicated and far more contested than it had been even when Defoe published *Robinson Crusoe* some fifty years earlier. Likewise, interest within the Anglican church and the Society for the Propagation of the Gospel in furthering American missionary efforts increased over the first half of the eighteenth century (see Cross), and that interest might be seen reflected in this novel.

The Female American ought additionally to be considered within the extraordinary transnational tradition of early eighteenth-century fiction produced about America and its social and cultural possibilities, a tradition that would include such other overlooked texts as the German and Dutch Robinson-ades,[1] Penelope Aubin's 1723 British Robinsonade *The Life of Charlotta Du Pont, An English Lady; Taken from her own Memoirs,*

---

1   See Blackwell for at least a partial listing of these texts.

and Alain-René Lesage's 1732 *Aventures du Chevalier de Beuchêne*, which incorporates an American Indian utopia and the character of a female missionary, and that was translated into English and printed in London in 1745.[1] If studies of women in the novel have so often been dominated by discussions of the domestic, it is texts like these that demand our attention if we want to uncover and understand this fascinating counter-tradition of anti-domestic female adventure.

---

1   For a study of Lesage's and other contemporary French novels, see Marouby.

A Note on the Text

There are three very nearly identical editions of *The Female American*. The first was printed in London in 1767, a second in Newburyport, Massachusetts c. 1800, and a third (clearly based on the Newburyport edition) in Vergennes, Vermont in 1814. In preparing this edition, which follows the original London edition, I have relied on a copy of the London text held at the Beinecke Library at Yale University, as well as on photocopy facsimiles of that edition. Comparisons between the London and the later American editions reveal only very minor differences between the three. The two American editions were published under the slightly different title of *The Female American; or the Extraordinary Adventures of Unca Eliza Winkfield*, and both use continuous chapter numbering in place of the London edition's separately paginated two volumes. These two editions include also occasional and minor modifications in spelling, punctuation, and paragraphing. When these changes are significant enough to alter or to clarify the reading or meaning of the text, I have indicated them in footnotes. I have silently corrected very obvious printer's errors, but have neither modernized nor regularized spellings, choosing to retain these elements of the original text. I have omitted the title page of volume 2, an announcement by the printers on a rise in rates for circulating libraries that appears at the end of volume 1, and a list advertising other titles available from the printers of this book that appears at the end of volume 2.

The inconsistent and confusing use of indirect discourse in *The Female American* deserves a more extended editorial explanation. All three editions of the novel frequently omit one or more of the sets of quotation marks that would typically distinguish direct from indirect discourse. As described above, these omissions become most complicated in the later chapters of the novel. Despite its confusion to readers, I have chosen, for reasons that are explained more fully in my discussion of narrative voice above (21-22), to preserve this style of the original and to supply clarifying footnotes.

While neither the footnotes nor the appendices are intended to be exhaustive, they are both meant to enable readers to consider and investigate further the novel's relationship to some of its more obvious and important sources. As *The Female American* becomes a more widely read and studied text, the number of these sources and our understanding of their role in the production and meaning of this novel will, I hope, continue to grow.

THE

Female American;

OR, THE

ADVENTURES

OF

UNCA ELIZA WINKFIELD.

COMPILED BY HERSELF.

IN TWO VOLUMES.

VOL. I.

LONDON:

Printed for FRANCIS NOBLE, at his Circulating
Library, oppofite *Gray's-Inn Gate, Holbourn*;

AND

JOHN NOBLE, at his Circulating Library, in
St. Martin's-Court, near *Leicefter-Square*.
MDCCLXVII.

ADVERTISEMENT.

THE following extraordinary History will prove either acceptable or not to the reader; in either case, it ought to be a matter of indifference to him from what quarter, or by what means, he receives it.

But if curiosity demands a satisfaction of this kind, all that he can receive is only this, that I found it among the papers of my late father.[1]

Upon a perusal of it, I found it both pleasing and instructive, not unworthy of the most sensible reader; highly fit to be perused by the youth of both sexes, as a rational, moral entertainment; and, as such, I doubt not, but that it will descend to late posterity, when, most of its contemporaries, founded only in fiction, will have been long forgotten.

The EDITOR.[2]

---

1 In both the Newburyport and Vergennes editions of the novel, this sentence reads: "But if curiosity demands a satisfaction of this kind, all that he can receive is only this, that I found it among the papers of a deceased friend."

2 In the Vergennes edition, this advertisement is signed not "The EDITOR" but "THE AUTHOR."

CHAP. I.

Motives for writing this history; discovery of Virginia; *the author's grandfather settles there; he is killed by the natives; his son is taken prisoner, but is saved by one of the king's daughters.*

THE following history of my life I never completely related but to one person; and at that time had no intention of committing it to writing: but finding the remembrance of it burdensome to my memory, I thought I might, in some degree, exonerate myself, by digesting the most material events in the form of an history; for which purpose I collected together such loose memorandums as I had occasionally made, which have enabled me to render the following relation more regular and complete than otherwise it could have been, had I been obliged to trust only to the power of recollection: how, and why, I afterwards came otherwise to dispose of it will appear in due time. The lives of women being commonly domestick, the occurrences of them are generally pretty nearly of the same kind; whilst those of men, frequently more vagrant, subject them often to experience greater vicissitudes, many times wonderful and strange. Though a woman, it has been my lot to have experienced much of the latter; for so wonderful, strange, and uncommon have been the events of my life, that true history, perhaps, never recorded any that were more so. However, I shall not endeavour to extort the reader's credence of them, if such my work should ever have any, by solemn professions of veracity; for, perhaps, they may never be read; but if they should, I think the greatest sceptic[1] will allow, uncommon as they are, that they do not exceed the bounds of probability. Here are two ends they cannot fail of answering, rational entertainment, and mental improvement. To proceed then:

The peaceful reign of king James I. of England[2] gave opportunity to the first attempt of the English to make a settlement in the Indies, at a place called, originally, Wingandacoa,[3] part of

---

1 Skeptic.
2 King James succeeded Queen Elizabeth in 1603 and reigned until 1625. The colony of Jamestown was established in 1607.
3 A number of early English explorers to Virginia, including John Smith, report that

the continent adjoining to Florida, called afterwards Virginia, in honour of our maiden queen Elizabeth, of blessed memory. As this place was first discovered by the great Sir Walter Raleigh, he obtained letters patent to settle a plantation there, *Anno Dom.* 1584. But it was some years after that time before any colony was sent there. The first plantation that proved successful, was began in 1607: at this time a colony arrived there of about an hundred persons, among the conductors of whom was Mr. Edward Maria Winkfield,[1] my grand-father; but as many of these died,[2] a further supply was sent the year after, under the care of captain Nilson; and again more in 1610, 1611, 1612.

In 1618, the settlement was thought of consequence enough to receive a governor from England. A very large colony arrived there two years after; and now the new-comers formed themselves into corporations. The first, and principal town, was honoured with the name of king James. But the happy prospect, with which the new-comers flattered themselves, was unhappily obscured by the native Indians, who came unexpectedly upon them, and massacred three hundred of them;[3] but this loss was soon repaired by a fresh recruit from England.—Thus much for the first peopling my native country.

The plantation which my grandfather first began, and which was the largest and most successful, devolved in a flourishing state to my father, Mr. William Winkfield, of whom I must relate a very extraordinary adventure, as it gave occasion to his growing more suddenly rich than he could have done by an

---

Wingandacoa is the native name for the country that the English renamed Virginia.

1 Edward Maria Wingfield was the first President of the Virginia colony. Amidst disputes caused in large part by a severe shortage of food, Wingfield was deposed and was succeeded, briefly, by John Ratcliffe, and later by John Smith. Wingfield recounts these events and defends himself in his "Discourse on Virginia." Winkfield is a variant spelling of Wingfield.

2 Percy describes these deaths in "Percy's Discourse of Virginia" (see Appendix B.2).

3 The 1622 massacre of the English colonists at Jamestown was led by Opechancanough, an uncle of Pocahontas. Accounts of the massacre are in Edward Waterhouse's *Declaration of the State of the Colony in Virginia* and John Smith's *Generall History* (see Appendix B.3.iii).

infant plantation, and gave birth to me; and in the consequences of it effected a more happy issue to my future adventures than could otherwise have happened.

At the time of the massacre, mentioned above, my grand-
father was killed, and my father, with a few more, was taken
prisoners[1] by the Indians; and as it was a very dark night, was
hurried along many miles before he could perfectly discover
any objects: at length the rising sun discovered to his view, at
some distance, a large river with a great number of boats on it;
into one of these he was forced, and then bound hand and foot.
In a little time all the boats were in motion, and for some hours
continued to go with great rapidity. My father had now but too
much time to reflect on his unpromising situation, and recalling
to his mind the words of his elder brother, whom he had left in
England, he thought them unhappily predictive.

He was a clergyman, and one of true piety and sound erudi-
tion. When his brother, my father, was about to quit England,
with their father, to settle in this new discovered country, "My
dear brother Bill," said he, "I know too well my duty to my
father to remonstrate against any action of his, though in secret
I may dread the consequence; but as I am your brother, and
your elder, I may presume to give my opinion; may it not be
prophetic! We have no right to invade the country of another,
and I fear invaders will always meet a curse; but as your youth
disenables you from viewing this expedition in that equitable
light that it ought to be looked on, may your sufferings be pro-
portionably light! for our God is just, and will weigh our
actions in a just scale."

My father at this time was about twenty years old, of a
remarkable fair complexion for a man, with brown hair, black
eyes, and was well shaped. I should not give a description of his
person, but that to it he owed, as it seems, his future preservation. The Indians continued their voyage about four or five
hours, when they stopped on the same side of the shore on
which they had embarked. As soon as they were landed, my
father, with five other English captives, tied one to another,

---

[1] The word "prisoners" does not appear in the Newburyport and Vergennes editions.

were drove, like sheep, many miles up the country, and then lodged in a cabin till next day; however, in the interim, they were plentifully supplied with dried Indian corn, dried goats flesh, and a kind of small wine, but thick, though well flavoured. They had heard that some of the Indians were men-eaters, and thought these were such, or that they would not have fed them so plentifully but to render them, as we do hogs, the better food: however, in this they were mistaken.

The next day, soon after sun-rising, my father and his five unhappy companions were brought out of their cabin; their cloaths[1] were taken off, and they placed in a circle formed by a great number of Indians of both sexes, all naked, except a small covering of foliage about their middle, which decently covered the distinction of sexes. This local covering of several of the females was composed of beautiful flowers. The unhappy captives stood amidst this assembly a considerable time, whilst a venerable old man seemed to address them in a pathetic manner, for tears accompanied his words. He was, as my father afterwards learned, their king, and of a very numerous people; and the purport of his long speech was this:

"Men, for I see you have legs, arms, and heads as we have, look to the sun," here he pointed up to that luminary, "he is our god, is he yours? He made us, he warms us, he lights us, he makes our corn and grass to grow, we love and praise him; did he make you? – did he send you to punish us? if he did, we will die, here are our bows and arrows, kill us." Saying this, they all threw their bows and arrows within the circle, between them-selves and the captives. Not then knowing their meaning, they stood silent; the king then continued his speech, "Our god is not angry; the evil being who made you has sent you into our land to kill us; we know you not, and have never offended you; why then have you taken possession of our lands, ate our fruits, and made our countrymen prisoners? Had you no lands of your own? Why did you not ask? we would have given you some. Speak." It seems they had no idea that there are more languages than one; therefore taking their silence for a confes-

---

1 Clothes.

sion of guilt, their king proceeded, "You designed to kill us, but we hurt no man who has not first offended us; our god has given you into our hands, and you must die."[1]

This said, the Indians took up their bows and arrows, whilst others bound my father and his five unhappy countrymen, and cut off the heads of the latter, one after another. My father expected the same fate; but just as the executioner was about to give the stroke, a maiden, who stood by the king, and whose neck, breast, and arms, were curiously adorned with jewels, diamonds, and solid pieces of gold and silver, and who was one of the king's daughters, stroked my father with a wand. This was the signal for deliverance; he was immediately unbound, and a covering, like that the Indians wore, was put round his body, and a kind of chain, formed of long grass, round his neck, of a considerable length, one end of which the princess took hold of, and gently led him along, till she came to a bower composed of the most pleasing greens, delightfully variegated with the most beautiful flowers; a shady defence from the sun, which then shone with uncommon heat. Beneath, was a large collection of leaves, which covered the whole surface of the ground to a great depth; here she made him sit, none present but themselves. She seated herself by him, viewed him with great attention from head to foot, felt his face and hands, but with the greatest modesty. She then arose, and going out returned presently with a cocoa nut shell, and drinking first, presented him the remainder of a liquor of most delicious taste, of the vinous kind; at the same time offering him a basket of various fruits. My father freely accepted of both, and found himself surprizingly refreshed. She then made a sign to him to lie down, and with looks of ineffable tenderness, retired; having first laid her bow and quiver filled with arrows by him, and fastened the door of the bower with a twig.[2]

---

1   For reports on the Indians' supposed sun worship, see Appendices B.1.i and B.2. Defoe also remarks on the Persians' practice of sun worship in *Serious Reflections* (132–34).
2   Smith's account of his reception by the Queen of Appomatox and his deliverance from captivity by Pocahontas are in Appendix B.3.iii.

This tender and extraordinary treatment had so far composed my father's mind, that, joined with the excessive heat of the day, and the wine together, he was so much overcome, that he insensibly fell asleep, amidst his reflections on this strange adventure. When he awoke, he found two Indian slaves fanning and defending him from the flies; which in that country are very hurtful. No sooner did they perceive he was awake, but one of his attendants withdrew, and presently returned, I cannot say with his fair, but with his black deliverer, who, smiling, gently pulled him by his chain, and led him, now willing and fearless, to a neighbouring cabin, greatly distinguished from those about it, both by its largeness and elegance.

Here he again saw the king, before whom he bowed; whilst his patroness presented the end of the chain she held to her father, who with much seeming affability returned it to his daughter. By this act my father understood he gave him as a captive to his daughter, who, immediately breaking the chain from around his neck, threw it at his feet, making a motion to him that he should set his foot upon it, which he having done, she clapt her hands, and cried out, *Hala pana chi nu*, "great peace be to you."

Though my father did not then understand her words, he could not but conceive her actions as declarative of his liberty; for actions are a kind of universal language: he therefore threw himself at her feet, when she in return offered him her hand to rise, and then led him into another cabin, completely furnished after the Indian manner. Here he found the two Indian slaves who had attended him in the bower: these the princess presented to him, and whom by the homage they paid him, he understood he was to consider as his slaves. His cloaths which had been taken from him, together with those of his less happy companions, were brought to him.

The princess continued some hours with him, and they participated of a collation of fruits, whilst the princess continually talked to him, as if he had understood her language. This agreeable society continued several weeks, she visiting him every day, shewing him the neighbouring fountains, woods, and walks, and every thing that could amuse. At last my father began to understand her language, which redoubled all her past pleasures, when, according to the simplicity of the uncorrupted Indians, she declared that love for him, which he had long before understood by her actions.[1]

Though a complexion so different, as that of the princess from an European, cannot but at first disgust, yet by degrees my father grew insensible to the difference, and in other respects her person was not inferior to that of the greatest European beauty; but what was more, her understanding was uncommonly great, pleasantly lively, and wonderfully comprehensive, even of subjects unknown to her, till informed of them by my father, who took extraordinary pains to instruct her; for now he loved in his turn: and sure he must have had a heart strangely insensible if such great kindness, joined with such perfections, had not had that effect.

They had now lived together six months, and understood each other tolerably, when Unca, for that was the princess's name, proposed their marriage. As she was a Pagan, though my father sincerely loved her, and wished for that union, he could not help shewing some uneasiness at the proposal. This the observant princess instantly saw. "What," cried she, "does not my Winka," so she called him, "love me?" My father caught her in his arms; "Yes, my dear Unca," cried he, "I do, but my God will be angry if I marry you, unless you will worship him as I do." This gave birth to a long conversation, in which, though my father was a very sensible man, and had enjoyed a good education, being very young, he found it not a little difficult to teach another what he yet firmly believed himself; but as we readily believe those whom we love, he was more successful than he expected, and in a little time the princess became convinced of her errors, and her good understanding helped to forward her conversion.[2]

Thus love and religion agreeably divided their time; and so

---

1 See Appendix B.3.iii for Smith's account of the love between John Rolfe and Pocahontas.
2 For Pocahontas's instruction in Christianity, see Appendix B.3.iii.

happy was my father with his princess, that he almost forgot his former situation, and begun to look upon the country he was in as his own, nor indeed did he ever expect to see any other again; and he now loved Unca as much as she did him, and was therefore willing to make her and her country his for ever; but an unexpected event soon gave a different turn to their affairs.

CHAP. II.

The king's eldest daughter conceives a passion for him, which produces disagreeable consequences, from which he is delivered by .

My father had never seen any other of the king's daughters since the day of his deliverance from death, but his dear Unca, till one day sitting in a wood to shelter himself from the excessive heat of the sun, the king's eldest daughter approached him. As soon as my father saw her, supposing she was one of the king's daughters, he arose to salute her with the profoundest respect. "Winca," said she, "I have long sought for such an opportunity as this; let us therefore retire further into this wood, that we may converse with more freedom." My father, unsuspecting the occasion of this visit, obeyed, when the princess thus began: "Winca, it is our custom to be silent, or to speak what we think; we are of opinion that nature has given us the same right to declare our love as it has to your sex; know, Winca, then, that I have seen you, and that the oftener I have seen you the more I love you; I know my sister loves you, but I am my father's eldest daughter, and as he has no son, whoever married me will be king after his death."

My father was so much surprized at this unexpected declaration, that he was not able immediately to reply; but as soon as he was a little recovered, he endeavoured to excuse himself as well as he could, by pleading his love and prior engagement to her sister; but it was in vain: all he could say tended but to provoke her anger. At last, in a rage, not to be described, she cried, "If you will not love me, you shall die; my sister shall never enjoy an happiness that I aspire to; nor shall my vengeance be long delayed; this instant shall put a period to your life." However menacing these words were, my father was not greatly alarmed, as they were uttered by an unarmed woman, and which he conceived to be only the effect of passion, and unluckily smiled. "What!" cried she, "do you scorn my love, deride my power? know wretch, Alluca can despise love and death at her will." Saying this, she clapt her hands together, and immediately six male Indians appeared from behind the trees, where they had stood at some distance unperceived by him.

"Seize that white infidel," cried she; and in an instant all power of defence or flight was equally taken from him. She then took a pomegranate-shell out of a kind of pocket that she wore by her side, and going up to a poisonous herb, squeezed the juice of it into it; then advancing to my father, "Here," said she, "be mine, or drink this; I offer you love and death; make your choice." "I can love none but Unca," replied he.

She then ordered four of the slaves to hold my father whilst the two others were about to force the poisonous draught into his mouth. "Hold," cried my father, "if I must die, I will drink it myself, I cannot do too much for Unca; she gave me life, and for her sake I will lose it – I drink Unca's health; her love shall make it sweet." He drank it, and I suppose the ministers of his intended death soon left him; for not long after he awoke, as it were from sleep, and found himself in the arms of his dear Unca, when in a languid tone he uttered, "What! do I meet my dear Unca so soon in another world? this was worth dying for." He then sunk again, as into a sleep.

It seems the princess Unca, having missed my father, arrived just after her sister and the slaves had retired, and saw him sink upon the ground. As she was no stranger to her sister's love for my father, her quick apprehension soon suggested what had happened; and as the Indians are remarkable for their knowledge of poisons, and no less so for their skill in antidotes, she instantly sought, and as quickly found, an herb whose salutary efficacy she was well acquainted with. She immediately squeezed the juice of it into his mouth, which soon reached his stomach, and made him eject the poison; but still his eyes were closed; a second dose revived him, and opening his eyes he uttered those words to the princess, just now related. "Heaven be praised," said the princess, "my dear Winka, that I came time enough to save a life dearer to me than my own; suck more of this juice, and you will be entirely recovered." He did so, and was soon able to get up and walk; but with a slow tottering pace, like a man whose brain has been hurt by the fumes of wine. The princess perceived his condition, and as they passed along gathered some flowers, the smell of which quickly dispelled the fumes, and fortified his brain so powerfully, that he was soon perfectly recovered, and his strength and understanding both entirely restored. Having returned the princess ten thousand thanks for thus giving him life a second time, they walked slowly homewards.

During their short walk, my father related to the princess Unca all that had passed between him and the princess Alluca, her sister. When he had finished his relation, the princess replied, "I will take effectual care for your security to-night, where my sister will not be able to discover you, and to-morrow I will consult my father what further measures we shall pursue." She then led him through some bye-paths of the wood, to the hut of an honest Indian, in whom she could confide; here she left him, with a caution not to stir out till her return next day.

Early the next morning the princess Unca, and her father, came to the hut where his daughter had concealed my father. Here a consultation was begun. The king said, "He could no more blame his eldest daughter than he did his younger, for loving my father; that Alluca had conceived an affection for him at the same time that Unca had, and at the instant that she touched him with her wand, Alluca was about to have done the same; that he highly condemned her intention to poison him; yet as she was tenderly beloved by him, as well as Unca, and his heir, he hoped my father would not desire him to inflict any punishment on her, since the loss of her lover would be a sufficient one." My father frankly declared that his regard for him, and his love for Unca, were sufficient motives to induce him to forgive her. The king then proposed that, to prevent all future danger, my father and the princess should be immediately married; and that they should both set out instantly for the place of my father's abode, and that, on his account, he would enter into a treaty of friendship with his countrymen; and added, that he would give him a portion worthy of a princess.

As my father considered marriage as a civil, as well as a religious, ceremony, and found, by their discourse, that their matrimonial ceremonies had nothing in them contrary to his own religion, he very readily consented. An Indian priest was sent for, and the ceremony was soon performed. A proper cabin, or hut, was immediately prepared for the reception of the new-married couple, and they were securely guarded, to prevent further mischief, till such time as the necessary preparations were made for my father's return, with his bride, to his own plantation. In a few days, every thing was ready for their departure. They took an affectionate leave of the old king, and got into a canoe provided for them, attended by several others, in which were several Indian maidens to attend Unca, and men slaves for my father, and a considerable baggage, the contents of which my father was then unacquainted with. Taking the advantage of wind and tide, they in a few hours arrived, without any accident, within a small distance of my father's plantation, to which he was heartily welcomed by his neighbours, who never expected to see him again. They were greatly surprised at his extraordinary adventure, and very glad that it proved the means of a friendship between them and the Indians.

My father being again settled with his dear Unca, in his own habitation, they were now married, according to the rights of the church of England, by an English chaplain belonging to one of the men of war that then lay in the harbour. Now they began to examine the presents that the king had made them, and found them to be very valuable, consisting of a great quantity of gold dust and precious stones, and many curiosities peculiar to the Indians. However, my father thought it prudent to conceal the greater part of his riches from the knowledge of his neighbours, not knowing how strong a temptation a display of them might prove, as many of the colony were not only persons of desperate fortunes, but most of them such whose crimes had rendered them obnoxious in their native country.

As my father had persuaded his wife to conform to the European dress, he provided for her as well as he could, till he had an opportunity of procuring cloaths more suitable to her dignity. He took every opportunity that offered to send part of his riches over to England privately, to be there disposed of, and such goods in return to be sent as he wanted; for it seems he had no inclination to leave his habitation, and the thoughts of it were highly disgusting to the princess: but had his own desires been ever so much for a removal, he would have sacrificed them to those of the princess, whom he passionately loved.

My father built him a more elegant house, which was suitably furnished, and his plantation by far the best and largest of any about him. This was a work of time. In the interim, my mother, proving with child from the night of their marriage, was safely delivered of me. I was, a month after, baptized by the name of Unca Eliza. The king, my grand-father, frequently sent a messenger to inquire after his children, who always attended with some present of fruit, flowers, or something more valuable. Thus happily did my father and mother live together, till I was about six years old; during which time they never heard the least news about their sister Alluca: but at this period an Indian brought the news of the old king's death, and that Alluca, still single, was received as queen.

A little after, as my father and mother were sitting in the garden, and I playing at their feet, a slave informed them that two Indians were come from the princess Alluca. As soon as they came into the garden my father was surprised to see that they had each of them a great coat on, contrary to the Indian custom: he had scarce made this reflection before one of them, being come close up to him, pulled a short dagger out of his sleeve, and made a push at him, which most probably would have proved mortal, had not he, by a sudden motion, avoided it. At the same instant my mother gave a loud shriek, when my father, turning his eyes, saw her falling with a dagger in her breast, for the other assassin had been too successful in his murderous attempt. My father caught her in his arms, and received her dying blood and breath together. The slaves, that my mother's shrieks and my cries had brought to us, presently seized the two murderers. One of them, who dearly loved my mother, drew the dagger out of her breast, and plunged it into the heart of him who had assassinated my mother, and was going to have done the same by the other, when my father cried out, as loud as he was able, "Take him alive." He was instantly bound hand and foot, and carried to a place of security.

What is human felicity? How often our greatest pleasures procure us the greatest misery! This moment behold a happy couple mutually endearing themselves to each other, whilst the infant offspring of their loves beholds their joys, partakes of, and adds to them. The next – but let the scene sink into darkness! 'tis too affecting for a daughter's pen to draw.

CHAP. III.

As soon as my mother was buried, and my father a little composed, he called for the surviving assassin, and from him learnt
that the princess Alluca had compelled him and his companion
to be the instruments of her revenge on them, for his having
slighted her love. My father consulted with the rest of the
planters, whether they should deliver the assassin up to justice,
or let him go home. Considering the infant state of the colony,
and the temper of the reigning princess, they thought it prudent to avoid every thing that might occasion a quarrel with
the Indians, and therefore agreed to give their prisoner his liberty. At his departure, my father charged the slave to tell his
queen, that her God, the sun, had seen the murder she had
commanded, and would revenge it.

It was not long after before my aunt the queen died of grief.
A little before her death, she ordered, that after her decease her
heart should be sent to my father with this message: "Receive
a heart that, whilst it lived, loved you, and had you received it,
it had never been wicked. Forgive my revenge, and let my
heart be buried with you when you are dead; but may the sun
give you many days!" This was accompanied with a very great
present of gold dust, and her bow and arrows, of exquisite
workmanship, for me. The bow, and some of the arrows, I still
have.

This renewed my father's grief, which had indeed but little
subsided; therefore to divert his sorrows, and give me a better
education, he determined to return to England. Every thing
was accordingly prepared. I was about seven years old when we
embarked, attended by several male and female slaves. We had a
tolerable passage to England, and found my father's brother in
good health. He was, as I before observed, a clergyman, and
had a living in Surry, where he constantly resided, had a wife,
one son, and three daughters, the youngest of them elder than

me. He was exceedingly glad to see his brother, and received me as if I had been a child of his own. He was an excellent divine, of great piety, and of uncommon learning, but ill provided for in the church. As my father was very rich, he gave him five hundred pounds for each of his children, and soon after bought the next presentation to a living of three hundred a year.[1] The incumbent dying soon after, he presented my uncle to it, with a thousand pounds to pay the expence of removing, as he said when he gave it. This occasioned our removal to a pleasant village near Windsor.

If I was kindly entertained by my uncle, I was little less caressed by the neighbours. My tawny complexion, and the oddity of my dress, attracted every one's attention, for my mother used to dress me in a kind of mixed habit, neither perfectly in the Indian, nor yet in the European taste, either of fine white linen, or a rich silk. I never wore a cap; but my lank black hair was adorned with diamonds and flowers. In the winter I wore a kind of loose mantle or cloak, which I used occasionally to wear on one shoulder, or to cast it behind me in folds, tied in the middle with a ribband, which gave it a pleasing kind of romantic air. My arms were also adorned with strings of diamonds, and one of the same kind surrounded my waist. I frequently diverted myself with wearing the bow and arrow the queen my aunt left me, and was so dexterous a shooter, that, when very young, I could shoot a bird on the wing.[2]

My uncommon complexion, singular dress, and the grand manner in which I appeared, always attended by two female and two male slaves, could not fail of making me much taken notice of. I was accordingly invited by all the neighboring gentry, who treated me in a degree little inferior to that of a princess, as I was always called; and indeed I might have been a queen, if my father had pleased, for on the death of my aunt, the Indians made me a formal tender of the crown to me; but I declined it.

---

1 Presentation is used here in its ecclesiastical sense; in other words, William Winkfield served as a patron for his brother, whom he successfully nominated for a benefice, or ecclesiastical office.

2 See the illustration of Unca Eliza Winkfield which precedes the introduction to this edition; see also Appendix A.1.ii and B.1.iii.

My uncle, who gave his daughters the same learned education with his son, desired I might make one of their society. This was very agreeable to my father, and no less so to me, who was very fond of my cousins, and willing to do what they did. I could already speak the Indian language as well as English, or rather with more fluency.

In this manner we lived near a year, happy I should say all of us, but my father, who, as he had no business to do, grew more melancholy: he therefore resolved to revisit the country where he had left the remains of his princess. It was in vain to intreat his stay, my uncle and aunt's remonstrances were lost, and only served to confirm his resolution of returning to his plantation. However, he thought proper to leave me with my uncle, to complete my education. Though I was unwilling to part with my father, I was as much so to leave my cousins, and therefore staid behind pretty contentedly. My father, before his departure, made great preparations for the improvement of his plantation, rather for his amusement, than from a desire of gain.

I continued here till I was eighteen years of age; during which time I made a great progress in the Greek and Latin languages, and other polite literature; whilst my good aunt took care of the female part of my education with equal success. Tawny as I was, with my lank black hair, I yet had my admirers, or such they pretended to be; though perhaps my fortune tempted them more than my person, at least I thought so, and accordingly diverted myself at their expence; for none touched my heart.

Young as I was, I often thought on my dear mother, and honoured her memory with many tears. And as I found it was the custom in England to erect monuments for persons who often were interred elsewhere, I desired my uncle to erect a superb mausoleum in his church-yard, sacred to the memory of my dear mother. It is a lofty building, supported by Indians as big as life, ornamented with coronets, and other regalia, suitable to her dignity. The form is triangular, and on one side is cut an inscription in the Indian language, containing a short account of her life and death. This I drew up and translated into Latin and English, which fills up the two other sides; on the top is an urn, on which an Indian leans, and looks on it in a mournful posture. The whole is surrounded with iron pallisadoes. This I often visited, and here I dropt many a tear.

My father, by this time, begun to think my absence long, and desired my return, which was equally agreeable to me; for though I was pleased with my situation, and the affectionate treatment of my relations, yet I secretly longed to see my native country, of which I retained a perfect idea, but more so to see my father. Every thing being prepared for my voyage, I, with my four slaves, embarked on board a ship for my return home, being then in my eighteenth year. However, my uncle insisted that his son John Winkfield, my cousin, should go with me to take care of me. His regard for me, and desire to see a strange country, made him very glad to accept of the proposal.[1]

During our voyage, my cousin neglected no opportunity to renew his address to me, which he had before begun in England. I gravely told him I would never marry any man who could not use a bow and arrow as well as I could; but as he still continued his suit, I always laughed at him, and answered in the Indian language, of which he was entirely ignorant; and so by degrees wearied him into silence on that head.

I shall not trouble my readers with any particulars of our voyage, and shall only say, that after a tedious and indifferent one, I once more found myself in the embraces of a tender father. The sight of me revived in his memory the remembrance of my dear mother, which drew from him a flood of tears, with which I sincerely joined mine. As soon as these subsided, his transports of joy were as great to see me returned in safety, and so much improved. He received my cousin with great affection, and, on his return home, gave him a bill on England for one thousand pounds sterling; which he might well do, for he was extremely rich. I on my part desired some considerable presents to be sent to my uncle and aunt, and to my cousins, with some of less value to my female acquaintance; together with some natural curiosities of my own country, as birds, shells, &c.

---

1   Robinson Crusoe's departure from England is described in Appendix A.2.i.

There was one circumstance attending my education, whilst under my uncle's tuition, that, in justice to his memory, I ought not to omit, the religious part; and in this he was as methodical and exact as though I had been to be a divine; nor did he inculcate religion as a mere science; but in such a warm and affecting manner, that whilst his lectures convinced the understanding, they converted the heart, and made me love and know religion at the same time. The happy effects of his pious instructions I have experienced throughout my life; and indeed in one part of it they were not only of the greatest comfort to me, but of the highest use; as will appear hereafter.

But to return to my father: neither his riches, business, nor even my company, whom he most affectionately loved, could cure him of that melancholy under which he laboured from the decease of my mother. This, at length, determined him once more to visit England, that new objects might divert his mind. With this view he soon found means to remove his great wealth to England, and prepared to dispose of his plantation; but by the time he had almost done the former, and had agreed to let his plantation, he grew so bad as to be incapable of removal, and in a few days went to that happiness in another world, which he could not enjoy in this.

CHAP. IV.

Unca buys a sloop, and embarks for England; the captain proposes a
match between her and his son; her slaves and attendants massacred,
and herself left on an uninhabited island.

HAVING paid my father every funeral honour I could, and
having nothing now to attach me to this country, and the bulk
of my great fortune lying in England, I determined to embark
for that kingdom, and to conclude my days in my uncle's
family. But Solomon saith, "The heart of man deviseth his way,
but the Lord directeth his going:" and so I found it.[1] I was now
in my four and twentieth year. At this time an opportunity
offered that favoured my intended voyage. There was a sloop in
the harbour, a good sailing vessel, and large enough to carry
me, my attendants, and effects. I chose an old captain, who had
lately been ship-wrecked, and lost his all, and who wanted to
get over to his son in England, to undertake the care of us, and
as, a gratuity for his trouble, promised, if we arrived safe in England, to give him the ship, that he might once more be able to
follow his occupation.

This proposal he accepted with great joy, and having got
together a sufficient number of hands to navigate our vessel, I
prepared to embark. Notwithstanding what my father had
before sent to England, I had yet a great many valuable goods
to take with me, to the amount of near ten thousand pounds.
These being safely lodged on board, I followed myself, attended
by my two favourite female slaves, who had sailed with me
before, and six men slaves, who begged to attend me; though I
had offered them their liberty, if they chose to stay behind.

We sailed with the first fair wind, and had not been on our
voyage above a day before the captain, willing to lose no time,
began to talk to me very freely about marriage. He did not
indeed sollicit me for himself; but he made strong courtship for
his son. I at first answered him with good humour, and told
him I hoped he would let me see his son before I determined

---

1   Proverbs 6:18.

to have him; and that if he could shoot with my bow and arrows, which then hung by me in the cabin, as well as I could, I would have him, were he ugly or handsome. But I soon found that he was too much in earnest, and I too much in his power: for in a peremptory manner he told me, that if I would not immediately sign a bond to marry his son, on our arrival in England, or forfeit thirty thousand pounds, I should neither see England, nor return to my plantation. I wondered he did not propose himself, but I found afterwards that he was a married man, as he informed me. I did not know law enough then, or else I might have given the bond, and so have avoided the distress that my refusal occasioned, as in equity I might have been released from the penalty; and the readier, as my two female slaves were witnesses to all he said. But as I persisted in my refusal, he grew incensed, and having I suppose gained the ship's crew by promises to assist him, at last told me he was come to a resolution, that as I persisted in my refusal, he was now very opportunely coming to an uninhabited island, where he would leave me to be a prey to wild beasts; and that as I had given him my ship, he would make bold to give himself the cargo. Two of my men slaves happened to come behind him just as he said these words, when one of them caught him in his arms, and the other opening the cabin-window, threw him into the sea. I know not whether I was sorry for this, at that instant; but I soon had occasion to be heartily so, for the consequence was fatal to them. As our ship, at this time made very little way, and the captain could swim, he presently got up to the ship, and being seen by some of the crew, who knew not how he got overboard, a rope was thrown out, and he quickly drawn up. In the mean time, one of the two men slaves went, and brought the other four into my cabin. Soon after the captain, and several of his men, armed with pistols and cutlasses, came into the cabin. The captain advancing up to him who threw him overboard, shot him dead, and now a terrible skirmish began. I indeed got no hurt, which was a wonder, for though no blow was aimed at me, the close[1] of the place exposed me to immi-

---

1 Closeness.

nent danger; and the two female slaves got several wounds. My men slaves were unarmed, and therefore soon overcome, three were killed outright, and the others, I suppose, mortally wounded. The poor faithful fellow who opened the cabin-window was hung up alive at the yard-arm, bleeding as he was, there to perish by hunger, thirst, and heat. This touched me more than my own misfortune, I offered the captain a thousand pounds to release him, and to let him be cured of his wounds. "Madam," returned the villain, "where are your thousand pounds? all you have on board is already in my possession."– Thus could I only pity, but not relieve.

I now expected my own destiny; and it soon arrived. The captain, who had left the cabin, to dispose of his prisoners, returned, and once more asked me if I would sign the bond? I answered, no; and at the same time desired that my two maids might have some care taken of their wounds. He replied, he had no surgeon, and if they did not grow well soon he should throw them overboard; but if they recovered, he should sell them the first opportunity: he then left the cabin. A few hours afterwards we came to an uninhabited island, where he put me on shore, for nothing that I said could soften his heart. I begged hard for both, or one, of my maids; but all the favour I could obtain, was my bow and quiver of arrows: indeed he gave me a box of clothes; but for these I did not thank him, as I never expected to use them, thinking myself consigned to some wild beast, whose prey I should become.[1]

---

1 Robinson Crusoe's shipwreck is described in Appendix A.2.i.

CHAP. V.

She offers up praise to God; takes refuge in an hermitage, where she
finds a manuscript left by the deceased inhabitant, in which are
instructions how to subsist on the island; reflections on her situation.

THUS disconsolate, and alone, I sat on the sea-shore. My grief
was too great for my spirits to bear; I sunk in a swoon on the
ground: how long I lay in this senseless state I know not, or
whether I might ever have recovered, had not a wave, brought
on by the rising tide, and which broke over me, awaked me. I
arose, hardly sensible where I was, or what I was doing, and ran
to a rising ground, and here I once again beheld my deplorable
condition. A few minutes recollection brought me to a sense of
my duty: for reflecting within my mind, that as the wicked captain could very easily have killed, or drowned me, it was a wonder that he should give me the least chance for life; that I ought
therefore to thank God for this escape, and to commit myself to
his providence. Indeed, in the hour of affliction we are ready
enough to pray to God for help; but are so taken up with a
sense of our miseries, that we forget that we have any mercy to
be thankful for. We should always sing a *Te Deum* before we
sigh a litany; for our sighs will sink before they reach heaven,
unless raised thither by the wind of praise.

Filled with these ideas I fell on my knees, and thanked God,
who had delivered me out of the hand of the wicked, and that
now I was in his only. On this occasion, these words of David
came into my mind; "Let me now fall into the hand of the
Lord, for his mercies are great, and let me not fall into the
hands of man." At the close of my prayers, I solemnly committed myself into the hands of God. I now arose from my knees
with a serenity by no means to have been expected. During
this composure of mind, I advanced to the highest ground I
could see, in hopes I might discover some place of safely, not
considering the improbability of such a discovery. Though the
sun shone very hot, which soon dried my wet clothes, yet I saw
it declining apace; I therefore kept looking about with eager
expectation, when at last I saw, or thought I did, the ruins of a

building. I advanced and saw it more distinctly: though it promised what I wished for, an asylum, yet I dreaded to go nearer. I looked, I stopped, I prayed, and then I moved again; thus strangely divided between hope and fear, I still kept going forward, and in an inexpressible agitation got close up to it, almost insensibly.[1]

I was so near now as to perceive a door half open: I listened and heard no noise. Fearful to retire, or to enter, I stood trembling a long time. How long I might have remained in this condition I know not, had not a sudden noise behind me, like the hallooing of a human voice, forced me precipitately to rush in, fearless of the danger within, that I might avoid that which threatened me from without. This double sense of danger deprived me of my senses, and I sunk down in a swoon. As I recovered by degrees, I saw all within the apartment before I was quite sensible enough to be afraid of my situation, and seeing nothing to alarm, I grew quite calm, and observing a kind of great chair, formed of several large and less stones, and the seat covered with a great heap of leaves, I sat down, and rested my weary limbs and agitated spirits.

The sun still shone pretty bright through the holes in the wall, which was of stone, and perfectly discovered every thing within. My fright had deprived me of the thought to shut the door: however, nothing came to hurt or alarm me. Before me was an heap of stones, on which laid a greater, which served as a table, and near enough to lean on. In a large fish-shell that lay on the table I perceived water, which I boldly ventured to drink of, and found myself instantly refreshed. I lifted up my heart to heaven, with thanks, and bespoke its further protection. On my right hand I saw a kind of couch formed, like a table, of a heap of stones, and the flat part, or surface, covered with moss and leaves. I now concluded that this was the habitation of some human being: but this gave me no alarm; for as I had read of hermits, who frequently retire from public life to enjoy their devotions in private, I imagined, from what I saw, that this must be the habitation of such a one, from whom I did

---

1 Crusoe's arrival on the island is described in Appendix A.2.ii.

not doubt but I should meet with protection and spiritual consolation.

This reflection restored me to such tranquility of mind, that I rested myself with the pleasing expectation of his return, which, considering it was near night, I thought could not be long. As I now had fresh cause to be thankful, I was so; and found I had spirits enough to sing a short Latin hymn of praise. But still no hermit appeared, and the sun was now set; but the moon was risen, and shone with so much brightness into the cell, that I scarcely missed the greater luminary. As I thus sat waiting, I observed a book lying on the table, which I had not before perceived, which I supposed to be a book of devotion; but on opening it, found it to be a manuscript, in the first leaf of which were these words.

"If this book should ever fall into the hands of any person, it is to inform him that I lived on this uninhabited island forty years; but now, finding the symptoms of death upon me, I am going to retire to another stone room, where I shall lay me down, and, if God pleases, rest for ever from all my troubles."[1]

As this was dated, as to the month and year, tho' without day of the month, I concluded he must be dead, as it was a month ago, and therefore gave over all expectation of seeing the hermit, with the thought of whose presence I had pleased myself. A little lower, in the same page, was added, "If thou shouldest be obliged to stay here any time, there are no wild beasts or noxious animals to injure thee; nor savages, except once a year, on one day, see page of this book, 397.[2] How you may subsist, you may learn from the history of my life."

I immediately turned to the page referred to, and found that it was yet two months to the time of the Indians coming on this island. I now thought I might sleep securely; I therefore shut the door, and fastened it with a heavy stone that lay there, I supposed for that use. Coming back from the door I spied an heap of Indian roots, which I presently knew to be such, and

---

1 See Longueville's *Hermit*, Appendix A.3. Defoe also discusses hermits and solitude in *Serious Reflections* (5-7).

·2 This reference to a specific page in the manuscript of the hermit is deleted in the Vergennes edition.

which serve instead of bread. As some of them were yet very good, and had been roasted, being very hungry, I ate heartily, and drank more of the water. As I walked about the room I saw in a nook another shell, which I imagined to be filled with the juice of wild grapes, from the look and taste, and therefore, as I was faint, drank some of it, but with caution, as I found it was grown strong with standing. As the moon shone very bright, I took out my Greek Testament, which I always carried in my pocket, it being my custom to read a chapter in it morning and night. I opened accidently in the epistle to the Hebrews, and the first words that offered to my view were these: chap. xiii. 5. *Οὐμήσε ἀνώ οὐδ᾽ οὐμήσε ἐνκαταλίπω*[1] I cannot but say they gave me great comfort, and I thought myself, in that moment, equal to all the difficulties I foresaw I had to encounter with, through the divine protection: though I very well remembered the caution my pious and judicious uncle gave me. "Beware," said he, "of the practice of some enthusiasts of our times, who make the word of God literally an oracle, by opening of it at particular times, and on particular occasions, presuming that where-ever they open, they are to apply the passage to themselves, or to the business they are about; because many have thereby been led into spiritual pride, and others into despair, as they opened on a promise, or a curse; whilst others have but too often, in the same manner, pleaded a warrant from scripture to perpetrate wickedness, or to propagate error.[2] Though," added he, "happy is the christian who by a prudent and rational use of the scriptures procures comfort to his soul. For as the apostle says, Whatsoever things were written aforetime, were written for our learning, that we through patience and comfort of the scriptures, might have hope." Rom. Ch. xv. v. 4.

Having read the whole chapter, and said my prayers, I prepared to take my rest on the stone couch, and laid down in my

---

1   *And be content with such things as ye have: for he hath said, I will never leave thee, nor forsake thee.* This translation of Hebrews 13:5 appears in place of the Greek original in both American editions. The Greek passage printed here follows that of the 1767 edition.

2   Baine explains that Defoe never condemned bibliomancy, the practice of "deliberately opening the Bible and relying upon God to direct the fingers and eyes to the appropriate page and verse," although it was generally criticized in his day (9-10).

clothes, with more composure, notwithstanding my dreadful situation, than my wicked captain, I think, could do, though indeed, I believe, a man may sin to such a degree, as to render his conscience quite callous; the most dreadful state a human being can sink into. Sleep soon closed my eyes, and I did not awaken till the sun was up. My spirits cheered by such timely refreshment, and my devotions performed, I quitted my cell, and directed my feet towards the sea-shore, to see what was become of my chest that I had left there the preceding night; little expecting to see it again, because I thought the working of the tide must have washed it into the sea, or have buried it in the sands. After some search, I spied it almost buried indeed in the sands, but was not much better for the discovery, as I was unable to remove it. I therefore returned to my cell, ate some of the Indian roots, and drank a little water, whilst my mind was busied, how I should break open my chest, and so bring away at times what I could not at once. I had indeed a small knife in my pocket, but that was not strong enough to cut through a thick board. I looked round my cell, but found nothing that could assist me. This gave me some concern, for if I could not come at my clothes, I considered that I should soon be very uneasy to myself, and started at the thoughts of going naked; however, for the present, I was obliged to be contented.

But now other cares came into my mind. The roots I fed on were not all of them good, but only a few of them so; and how was I to get more? I did suppose they grew in the island; but I was not fond of rambling. Though the hermit's manuscript assured me there were no inhabitants nor animals to hurt me, yet the thought of wandering alone was terrifying. I might lose my way, and not be able to find my cell again, or not under a long time; and even should I find plants near my habitation, how was I to make a fire to roast them? Other anxious thoughts still pressed upon my mind one after another. At last, I recollected, that in the memorandum I had read the night before, I was informed, that the hermit's manuscript contained instructions how to subsist. This once more cheered my mind; and I now began to give it a careful reading, but not regularly; impatiently looking here and there for those things that most concerned me. It was written in a fair legible hand. I soon found that there was a flint and steel in the cell I was in; that at some distance there was a small river that ran quite through the island; that he made use of the shell of a certain fish for a lamp, in which he burned the fat of goats, and for a wick made use of a particular reed. I then searched to learn how he got goats to supply himself with fat, and, at last, met with this memorandum: "When I first came upon this island, I found plenty of goats, yet having no fire-arms, I was never the better for the discovery, as they were too wild to catch. But observing that they were very fond of a yellow fruit that grows on several of the trees here, and that they were continually watching when any of it fell off to eat it, this suggested a thought, that if I gathered some of it, I might possibly tame them by giving them plenty of it to eat. I accordingly broke down some of the branches, and whilst I held them in my hand, they would follow me up and down like a dog, so that I could catch them when I pleased. I found also that the goats, if I laid plenty of this fruit before them, would let me milk them whilst they fed. I from this time, no more wanted either milk or goats flesh. But as I knew this fruit would not be on the trees all the year, I gathered large quantities of it in the season, and saved them to serve in the other part of the year."

This information gave me great pleasure; I immediately searched and found the steel and flint, and near them dry leaves and touch-wood. I now thought of setting fire to one end of my box, as thinking it better to burn part of my clothes than come at none of them: but however, I declined this method, in hopes of finding some better expedient; but was still very uneasy, lest the tide should remove it into the sea, or bury it out of sight in the sands; but I was obliged to run every risk. A few days afterwards what I wished for was effected by a means that I at first thought would have entirely deprived me of my chest. I was walking near the sea-side, looking at my chest, when I observed the sea to rise, and presently the winds blew very tempestuously. I retreated back enough to observe the storm in safety, which, at last, became very great, and soon saw my chest tossed about by the waves, as though it had been as light as a feather. I expected that every fresh wave would remove it for ever out of my sight; but it was removed further and further on shore, as the sea advanced, till, at last, I saw it no more. I then gave it up for lost, and returned home, for so I now called my cell, very uneasy.

However, the next day, the storm being over the night before, and the sun shining very bright, I again visited the shore, and the spot where the chest had lain, but in vain. But seeing at a distance higher up from the shore some rocks, my curiosity led me to go up to them, not with any expectation of finding my chest, for I had given over all thoughts of it; but climbing up one of them, I found my chest lodged there. I was glad to see it, though the same difficulty still remained, how to open it. Being weary with climbing the rock, I sat myself down to rest. As I was sitting on that side of the rock that declined to the sea, I observed that on the other side of the rock was a very deep descent, at the bottom of which were craggy stones, but level with the rest of the island. I was startled at my nearness to it; however, this suggested something to my mind. If, thought I, I could push the chest down this precipice, the fall might break it; at least, it would be out of the reach of the sea. However, I was afraid to do so, lest I should tumble over with it. But after some consideration, I thought that if I laid myself down on the ground, on the side on which I got up, I might attempt it. I accordingly tried, and with great difficulty moved it, but not immediately; at last, after a great deal of labour, it fell over. The noise it made, when it came to the ground frightened me, though I knew what it was. My next business was to get down the way I came up, and then to find my way to the valley. I did so, but was obliged to go a great deal about. When I was come near to the spot, I found the ground so rugged, that it was with great difficulty, and not without several falls, that I reached the chest, which I found broke into a great many pieces, and it took me up near a whole day to remove the contents; gowns, linen, and many other useful things. All these I conveyed to my cell; not a little pleased that I had, at last, conquered this difficulty, and was now supplied with things that I should have greatly wanted.[1]

But to return to where I left off: having found the steel and flint, I immediately made a trial of them, and they were in very good order. I found three lamp-shells ready prepared; I lighted them, and they burnt very well. My next attempt was to get some goats milk, as I had yet tasted nothing but roasted roots and water; I took a large fish-shell, of which I found plenty ready to my hand. It was not long before I met with the tree with the yellow fruit, and several goats under it, who ran a little way off as I advanced, but not out of sight, but seemed to wait as if they watched me. I found it very difficult to climb the tree; but, at last, got up and broke several boughs off: and as soon as I was down, the goats came to me; I laid the boughs down, and clapt my foot on them, lest the goats should drag them away. I now tried to milk one of them, but very aukwardly [sic], having never done so before. However, I got enough to drink then, and to bring home for another time. I repeated this practice till I became very ready at it; and not knowing how soon the fruit might fail, I took care to gather and save a good deal of it.

My next attempt was to kill a goat, as I found I grew weak for want of more substantial food than plants and milk. There was a knife fit for this purpose in my cell, and several others, and forks; but the thoughts of killing shocked me, and I was afraid to kill one whilst the others saw me, lest they should be afraid, and shun me for the future. Having therefore thrown down a good deal of the fruit, with a bough of it, I enticed one of them to follow me till out of the sight of the others; and then, but with great uneasiness to myself, killed it. But a more difficult task was still behind, to skin and cut it up; but as my time was not very precious, I had enough to bestow on it, and, at last, completed my job, though in a very bungling manner. I carried it home, and made a fire, having plenty of wood, and roasting some of it, I made a hearty grateful meal. What I could not eat whilst it was fresh, I salted; for I found plenty of salt on the rocks by the sea-side.

---

1   See Appendices A.2.ii and A.3 for other accounts of recovered chests from ship-wrecks.

My next care was to provide a new stock of roots, as those I found in the cell were nearly consumed. It was not long before I found plenty; these I roasted on a fire, and laid them up. If I was now rich in provisions, I was quickly more so; for almost every day, looking into the hermit's manuscript book, I learned from thence that there was not only plenty of shell-fish on the shore, all of them wholesome, except the black flesh kind, but that every tide left great numbers of other fishes in the holes and shallows. I soon tasted some of each sort, and found them very delicious; particularly a shell-fish, like what are called oysters in England, and which needed no dressing; others were of the lobster and crab kind; the shells of the latter, being large, were very useful. Besides fish and flesh, I could also help myself to birds of various kinds, particularly some like larks, which I took according to the hermit's direction in this manner. From several of the trees issued a kind of glutinous matter, which I gathered and besmeared the little low brambles and bushes with it, and by that means catched a great many small birds, that used to eat the berries of them.

What a plentiful table was here, furnished only at the expense of a little trouble! This happiness I owed to the misfortunes of another; for had not the hermit made these discoveries, and left the means of my coming at the knowledge of them, how miserable must have been the state of a lonely woman! Doubtless I should soon have perished with hunger! How graciously does the goodness of providence often raise help to the distressed from the misfortunes of others! The hermit who made these discoveries, and by them was supported, had great reason to thank God, and I no less cause to be thankful to the same being who influenced his heart to leave behind him the history of his life, which proved the preservation of mine.

If this reflection gladdened my heart, it was succeeded by one that gave me no less pain: "At last," cried I, "he died! – died here! – what might he not feel for want of some kind friend to ease his sufferings in his last hours! Forty years without human society! – no opportunity offered to restore him to his native, or to any other country! – must this be my fate?" Tears gushed from mine eyes, and sorrow filled my heart. Thus weeping and lamenting I sat, and from time to time exclaimed, Wretched princess! what have I done to suffer thus from human treachery? But at length, a more comfortable view of my condition again presented itself to my mind, and I was consoled: for I again reflected on the great improbability that there was of my finding such a resource in my captivity, as the hermit's book, and how thankful I ought to be. I will take this, cried I, as an earnest of a future deliverance. At this instant, I experienced such an inward persuasion in my mind, that I should escape from this island, that every uneasy thought fled, and left my mind a calm, scarcely to be expressed. I therefore arose, and went cheerfully about my little concerns; but not without having first thanked that God who had given me this consolation.

CHAP. VI.

The thoughts of her distress occasion a severe fever; recovers; seeks comfort in her own reflections.

As I had now settled my manner of living, I was very easy on that head, till this reflection destroyed all my peace: 'Tis true, I am well provided for the present; whilst the summer and fine weather continue, I can, with little difficulty, or rather amusement, supply myself with fish, flesh, and fowl; but winter no doubt will come, and how severe that season may prove I cannot foretel. How shall I, during the inclemency of it, procure the means of subsistence? There will be less plenty of birds; the gum, which now spontaneously issues from the trees, will then fail, the sands on the coast being more frequently and violently agitated, will be unsafe, and my supplies from thence less, perhaps none; the goats will also yield little or no milk; and the rain perhaps may continue for many days, nay weeks, and confine me entirely to my cell. – Such were the anxious perplexing thoughts that agitated my mind; and the fear of the future destroyed the enjoyment of the present. – I sat dissolved in sighs and tears, and indulged my melancholy, till the night drew on, when I laid me down, but not to rest; and so greatly was my mind afflicted, that it brought on a violent fever, attended with a delirium. I raved, I cried, I laughed by turns. I soon became so weak, that I was scarce able to crawl from my bed to get some water, of which I happened to have plenty. As my thirst was great, I drank freely of it; but as the fever continued three days, I was now reduced to my last shell-full of water. I had at this time an interval of sense, when I found I was too weak to go out of my cell to fetch more, yet my thirst forced me to drink this; which I did supposing it would be my last, and that death must be my next potion. I soon emptied the shell, and as well as I was able, and with as much resignation as I could, laid me down to die. It was not long before I fell asleep for the first time since the fever came on me; how long I slept I could not tell, but awoke in a great sweat, and found my thirst as great as ever, and to such an intolerable degree, that I determined, if possible, to attempt going to the river to drink, though I died in the way; for death itself was more eligible than the thirst I suffered. With much difficulty I raised myself up, and got upon the ground; but was obliged to crawl upon my hands and feet, and to rest very often by the way before I reached the river. Surely deliverance itself could not have given me greater pleasure than the sight of the water; I greedily thought there would be scarce enough to assuage my raging thirst. I laid myself flat on the edge, and whilst I drank, had the additional pleasure of cooling my hands and face.

At length, my thirst was happily allayed; but the river was not dried up. The coolness of the water was so agreeable to my hands and face, that I thought I would wash my feet, as they burnt with no less fierceness. To do this, I was obliged to seat myself on the bank. It was with much labour and difficulty I did so; but had scarce placed myself, when either the bank broke down, or I slipt, and into the water I fell, and plunged all over. Whether the water by its coolness braced my nerves, and gave me strength, or how I know not, but I soon reared my head above the surface, and crawled upon the shore; when my weakness again returned, and I fell all along, unable to stir, expecting to die every moment. At last, I fell into a deep sleep, I suppose for some hours, when I awoke in a violent sweat; I was still thirsty, but not so painfully as before, and even found myself refreshed. I was fearful to have recourse to the river, lest I should fall into it again, when observing a she-goat asleep, very near me, I made shift to creep softly to her, and sucked her dugs, which she happily permitted. This was at first a comfortable relief; but I soon after grew very sick, and vomited violently. But I found that my fever was quite gone off, and that I was no longer thirsty. Reflecting on the great escape I had from drowning, and the favourable change in my health, whereas the mere circumstance of being immersed in the water, in the condition I was, might have proved instant death, I lifted up my heart unto God, and unfeignedly thanked him for his mercy.

I now attempted to get up and crawl to my cell; but found myself too weak to do either. All I could do was, to sit up sometimes a little. The sun, indeed, dried my clothes apace, but its heat was too violent to bear long; I was forced therefore to crawl a little way off under the shade of some trees that grew on the banks of the river; but this I was long performing, though not above two or three yards off. The shade of the trees protecting me from the sun's scorching beams, and the cool breezes which came upon me from the river refreshing me greatly, I once more fell asleep. When I awaked I was greatly but agreeably surprised to find how much better I was. My clothes were quite dry; and now I hoped I might be able to get to my cell; for I saw the sun was setting: though I was not thirsty, I could have been glad of some more milk, but there was no goat near me; for notwithstanding the milk had made me sick, yet I believe it contributed to my recovery, by clearing my stomach. I once more attempted to crawl home, for I could do no more, and glad was I to do so. At last, I reached my cell, much fatigued and very weak, and greatly in want of some refreshment. I soon recollected there was some of that wine left that I drank of the first day I came, and made shift to reach it, but having no water to mix with it, I drank but a very little of it, and that little was too strong for my stomach to stay in it. Still finding my stomach empty and uneasy, I, at last, remembered my root bread, I cut a slice of it, and soaked it in the wine; I ate sparingly of it, and found it agreed with me, and refreshed me greatly. The rest of it I laid by my couch, and bit a piece of it now and then, for I lay awake most part of the night, but free from both thirst and fever.

Towards morning I slept soundly, and when I awaked I was much surprised to find how my strength was recruited, or rather my weakness abated. I got up, and most heartily thanked God for my recovery, and with the help of two sticks made shift to walk, though slowly. I reached some of the yellow fruit with which I used to entice the goats, and laid it before the door, in hopes, that the goats would see it, for I could not walk in search of them; putting some stones upon the boughs, that they might not drag them away. At last a she-goat came, and I milked her, and drank a large shell of it, with a little bit of my root bread. This agreed extremely well with my stomach; I continued this practice for about a week, once a day, drinking a little wine with water; and thus once more happily recovered my health and my strength to such a degree, that I could now walk about and do my little business; and, in a week more, was as well and almost as strong as before. I now had been upon this place a month; for as I had an Almanack with me, I kept an exact account of time, that I might be sure to conceal myself on the day the Indians were to arrive, as cautioned by the hermit's manuscript.

Being thus recovered, I could not but reflect that I owed my late sickness to my giving way to those anxious corroding cares that had arisen in my mind concerning my future subsistence; and I could not but condemn my folly, and mourn for the sinfulness of it, and of which, I hope, I heartily repented.

My dear uncle was a great recommender of meditation: "That man," said he, "hardly knows that he is a thinking being, who does not often meditate by himself. It is," said he, "a glorious privilege, and he who practices it will grow wiser and better by an hour's serious meditation than by a month's reading." "We should," continued he, "be often inculcating upon our minds the truths we know, and they will become fixed. We should often rebuke, advise, and console ourselves, and we shall become better men, more prudent, and more contented." I was so strongly convinced of the reasonableness and utility of this practice that I adopted it. And, according to his further advice, used to talk to myself aloud, as the occasion required, as I would to another; and that with all the force of argument, vehemence, and energy of expression I could, or as the nature of the subject required. Upon these occasions I have been frequently surprised to find how my understanding has been convinced, my affections moved, and my will determined. I have assented to a truth I never before believed, wept at the conviction of a fault, and have found a consolation in a time of trouble that I did not expect. On these occasions, it was always my custom to imagine to myself that my uncle was speaking to me; this I thought, as it were, inspired me, and gave an energy to my words, strength to my arguments, and commanded my attention. I have sometimes indulged this reverie to such a degree that I have really imagined, at last, that my uncle was speaking to me.

By reflecting on my late sickness and the occasion of it, I was led into one of these soliloquies; and thus in the imagined person of my uncle did I address myself.

"In vain, I find, are the precepts that I so often inculcated on your mind; they have not reached your heart, and, I fear, are erased from your memory. It was easy in the day of prosperity to hear instructions how to bear adversity, but in the hour of calamity they are forgotten. From the days of your infancy the smiles of providence almost constantly attended you. You were too young at your mother's death long to feel her loss; and that of your father's was the most poignant. Indeed, to be at once deprived of your great affluence, and secluded from human society, are afflictions not of a light weight. But still, could you find no consolation? The dread of approaching winter, in your situation, might alarm; but sure, at your first coming on this island, you had no less reason, surely more so, to be alarmed for your then immediate preservation. Yet what favourable circumstances have intervened! And such as, if properly improved, may prevent the calamities you dread. How preferable is your condition to that of those consigned to slavery for life! forced to bear with accumulated evils, utterly unknown to you! slaves to a tyrant, and the subjects of unrelenting cruelty! Ah, Eliza! would we but compare our sufferings with those of others, where would the wretch be found who would not have something wherewith to console himself?

"How many have voluntarily quitted the advantages of society, to avoid the temptations of it, in a worse retirement than yours? – Thus might I reason with a heathen, and I think, not without success. But is not Unca a christian, or would be such? Receive then the instructions of a higher school, and learn of a better master. Remember him who through sufferings was made perfect, and that the disciple is not to be above his master. Let then your whole life be one continual Ἀφορῶντες εις την Ιησοῦν.[1] The greater your calamities, the greater should be your trust and confidence in God. He who relies most on his provi-

---

[1] *Imitation of Jesus.* The American editions replace the Greek passage with this translation. The Greek passage printed here is consistent with that of the 1767 edition, except that the orthography has been updated.

dence, glorifies him most. We should never neglect the use of means whilst in our power: but when they fail, we must still look up to him, who needs them not; for when we have done our utmost, we must not despair, as though God's power was cut off with ours. No; at such a time we must commit ourselves and our wants to him, with a firm persuasion that he will help us. If we make him the object of our faith and prayers, we shall become the subjects of his mercy. Remember godliness hath the promise of this life, as well as of that which is to come. But always be mindful that we are to commit ourselves to him by a patient continuance in well-doing. – No imaginary flights of faith will warrant our confidence in him, nothing will do unless we prove ourselves to be his servants by keeping his commands; for true saving faith always produces good works. Believe and obey; be thankful to God for the mercies you enjoy, and trust in him for those you want. The citizen may be wretched and the solitary happy. Human felicity or misery is confined to no place or circumstance of life. The servant of God is safe wheresoever or howsoever he be. Humble thyself therefore, under the Almighty hand of God, and he shall exalt thee in due time. Let not your care for this present life make you neglect that of a future one. Should your body die here, your soul will not find the way to heaven the more difficult. Though the cloud of affliction now hangs over your head, the sun of mercy behind may dispel it, and once more show his glorious face. Believe, obey, and trust, and be saved, blessed, and delivered."

Thus did I endeavour to fortify my heart, and to learn patience and resignation to the dispensations of providence; nor were my attempts in vain; nor did I ever again suffer such anxious cares as those from which I was just now delivered. Submission or hope, one or both, were ever in a less or greater degree my solace.

CHAP. VII.

*Again consults the hermit's manuscript; some account of his life; finds
the hermitage to be the temple of the sun; discovers a great number of
mummies, and on her return from exploring the temple, perceives the
hermit at his devotions.*

I HAD not yet read the hermit's manuscript regularly, but here
and there, as I hoped to find some necessary and useful directions for my manner of subsistence. But having now pretty well
attained this desirable end, I purposed to read it from the beginning regularly through, without omitting any part. But before I
begun, for I found it would take up a great while, I once more
hastily looked it over, to find when, and what kind of winter I
had to expect. I found that it was now but the beginning of the
summer, or rather spring, and that I had at least six months certain good weather before me, except some great storms of
thunder and lightning. As I had so much time between me and
winter, I did not stop now to learn how the hermit provided
against that event; but, according to my first intention, assigned
a few hours every day to the history of his life.

As I have this manuscript still in my possession, I shall do no
more than give a very short view of its contents, though the
whole of it would very well deserve to be made public. From
this manuscript I learned, that the hermit as I called him, on
account of his recluse life, might yet be more properly called so
on account of his extraordinary piety. This history of his life is
indeed wonderfully extraordinary, highly entertaining, and full
of improvement. The first thirty years of his life were unhappily consumed in more than useless follies; in vices that had well
nigh brought him to a shameful exit, but ended only in the loss
of his liberty, which he very unexpectedly and no less wonderfully regained; if his living the last forty years of his life in this
place may be called a state of liberty.

But his residence here proved the happy means of his conversion, of which with great modesty and ingenuousness, he
gives an ample account. The manner of his living here was
attended with a greater variety of events, than could have been

expected from such a solitary situation. His occasional reflections are sensible and pious, useful and pertinent. This cell, as I called it, that I now inhabited, I found to be but one of many others; the ruins, as he rationally conjectured, of some very ancient palace, or rather temple, which he supposed anciently belonged to a very large statue, or image, at a considerable distance from the place of my habitation, and to which the ruins approached, and in part surrounded. This he imagined to have been an ancient idol sacred to the sun, which the Indians adored. For, says he, "Once a year, vast numbers of them come over from the continent in canoes, on the opposite side of the island, and having spent almost the whole day in a kind of devotion to this idol, they then go back again, and never revisit it till the annual return of the same day." The knowledge of which he having learned, he took such effectual care to conceal himself, that he never was discovered, as I afterwards was certainly satisfied. The latter part of his life was uniformly the same to the time that he wrote the memorandum already mentioned, which says, That he was retired from the cell he usually inhabited, to die in some other.

I had not patience to go through the whole history, till I had seen this extraordinary idol. For this purpose, I got up early the next morning, put some roots in my pocket, and a shell to drink out of, that I might have the whole day at my command. I could not, indeed, but have observed before, that there were many other stone rooms besides that which I inhabited; but had never as yet gone into any other excepting two; in one of which I laid up the branches of yellow fruit I gathered for the goats, and the other in which I kept my dried goat's flesh, and some dried fish. Upon searching, I found some uninhabitable, others in as good condition as that I dwelt in, some well lighted with holes on the sides, others dark. But being curious to see if I could discover why this distinction was made, not being far from my cell, I fetched one of my lighted lamps.

The first room I entered, I found surrounded with mummies, like those I have read of in the histories of Egypt, and one of which I once saw in England. At first I started; but instantly recollecting, that I had no cause to fear, I examined them with great attention. They were all placed upright, as close as they could be round the cell, without touching one another. Observing Indian characters upon each of them finely painted, besides various drawings of birds, beasts, insects, and other things, I examined them more nicely. As I understood the Indian languages perfectly, I soon learned that these had been priests of the sun. Each mummy had on it the name of the priest, his age, and the time of his death; by which I found that most of them had been there at least one thousand years. Leaving this, I went into another, and another, till I had visited a dozen, all filled in the same manner, with the same order of men, all uninjured by time.[1]

Some other rooms, which were much more spacious, were filled with stone coffins, with just room to pass between, and against the walls they were placed, at a little distance between each, to the height of four coffins. These I supposed had not been embalmed, for as they were all uncovered, I could see no remains of their bodies but the ashes; but at the head of each, lay a kind of coronet. I took up several of them, and imagined they were made of gold, as I afterwards found they were. I suppose, from the make of them, they had been worn upon their heads.

I should have observed that when I was viewing the mummies, I found golden coronets placed upon each of their heads, but of a larger and different make, which showed that they had never been worn, but made on purpose, as I conjectured, for the use to which they were applied. I was very desirous to know who those had been whose ashes only remained, and at last, discovered an inscription on the headstone of each coffin, from which I learned that they had been virgins of the sun, consecrated to the service of the temple. Of these virgins I found in different rooms many hundreds, and several hundreds of the priests. As I continued my search, I found other rooms, but all at a little distance from one another, some not at all injured by time, others a little, and some a great deal. At last, I came to a group of, I believe, about five hundred, of a different form from the rest, and much less. Each of these contained

---

1   Descriptions by Europeans of Native American embalming and mortuary practices in colonial Virginia appear in Appendices B.1.ii and B.3.ii.

only one mummy, which, upon inspection, I found were the mummies of the high-priests of the sun. These had also a crown of gold on their heads, and suspended on their breasts, a golden figure of the sun, rudely carved in gold. What a collection of mummies and of golden treasure! "But what is this?" cried I, "I had too much gold before to be happy." This reflection gave birth to a sigh; but I soon suppressed its progress; and as I found the day was too far gone to pursue my journey to the idol, I returned ruminating on what I had seen, towards my solitary cell; for such I must still call it, though I might truly say to my apartment in the palace. I should have mentioned that in each of the dormitories, I found a lamp of gold suspended from the roof; one of these was still burning. This confirmed what I had read of the perpetual lamps of the ancients.[1]

I had indulged myself so long in my rambles among these dormitories, that it was dark before I reached my cell. But what was my astonishment when pushing the door open, I saw in my cell a light! This, at the same instant, discovered to my sight, a venerable old man, with a long beard, kneeling as at his prayers. I concluded, that it must be the ghost of the old hermit. This was too much; and I sunk down in a swoon. My fall, I suppose, alarmed the hermit; for, when I came to myself, I found him sitting by me, supporting me in his arms, being too weak to lift me up. As soon as he saw me revive, "My daughter," said he, "be comforted, you are safe; whatever misfortune may have brought you here, what protection and help a poor feeble old man can give, you may depend on."

Being a little more composed, I got up, and accompanied the old man into the cell; though not as yet thoroughly satisfied whether I conversed with the dead, or the living. In the mean time he brought the shell that had still some wine in it to me; I drank a little of it, and found myself quite recovered, when we entered into discourse. He then drank some himself.

"Holy father," said I, "I thought you had been dead some weeks ago; are you really living, or do I converse with a spirit?"

---

1   Fires and flames that were kept continuously lit are a significant ancient symbol and element in a number of ancient rituals and traditions. This reference to "the perpetual lamps of the ancients" appears to be to the general tradition rather than to a particular use or text.

"My daughter," returned the hermit, "I am really a living body, though too weak and faint to live much longer. But how comes it that you speak to me in a manner as if you knew me? I was surprized to see you here, but more so to hear you talk in this manner; and, did not your late swooning convince me that you are a mortal like myself, I should think that I, in my turn, was also discoursing with a spirit."

This gave me occasion to acquaint him with the cause of my coming on the island, and what had passed since, to the time of our meeting.

"Have I then," cried he, "been so happy as to have my misfortunes prove the means of affording assistance to an innocent and unhappy sufferer? Thanks be to God! – I wrote," continued he, "the memorandum of my supposed approaching death, that you have read, and thinking my end to be very near, walked out with a design to go to one of the dormitories belonging, as I find by your information, to the virgins of the sun, in order to clear one of them of the ashes it contained, and lay myself down in it; and there to await my approaching dissolution, which I thought could not then be far off; but as I was going thither a kind of delirium seized my brain, and I wandered up and down, unknowing where I went. Though I had intervals of sense, they never continued long enough for me either to find my way back to my cell, or to a dormitory. The only advantage I reaped from them was when I found myself hungry or dry, to gather fruits to eat, and to seek for water. I suppose in my rambles I got to the more remote part of the island. Once indeed I imagined I was very near my cell, and that I thought I saw the figure of a woman standing at the door; upon which I halloed as loud as I could; but it vanished like lightning from my sight. Having to-day the enjoyment of my senses, I at the close of it found my way to my cell; there was just light enough to guide me to one of my lamps, which I lighted, and was kneeled down to say my prayers, when the noise of your fall made me turn round in a start, and I beheld you lying on the ground. This augmented my surprize, and it was some moments before I could recover myself, so as to be able to move to your assistance."

CHAP. VIII.

The hermit dies; the idol of the sun described; discovers a subterranean cell, that leads to the inside of the idol; a terrible tempest.

FINDING the hermit stopped his discourse, I told him, I believed that he really saw me, for that about a month ago, as already related in the foregoing part of my life,[1] the day I was put upon the island, as I stood at the door of his cell, fearful to enter, I then imagined that I heard an human voice calling to me: the fright drove me into the cell; but from that time to this I could never account for it, but concluded afterwards that the noise existed only in my fearful imagination.

During our conversation we refreshed ourselves with some goats flesh and roots, and, now the night being far spent, I persuaded the hermit, after much intreaty, to repose himself on the stone couch, whilst I sat in the chair. The sun was far advanced the next morning, when I found the hermit still reclined on the couch. I thought he might still be sleeping, and went softly out, to get some goats milk for our breakfast, and after my return waited some hours for his awaking; but as he did not stir, I began to suspect he might be dead. At last I persuaded myself to go nearer, and now perceived he was really so. I was sorry so soon to have lost his society, from which I promised myself much solace. As it was impossible for me to remove him, had I been ever so desirous, I immediately set myself to convey every thing out of the room into another, which I found equally convenient; only I had the trouble to gather moss and leaves to lay upon the couch.

When I quitted the room entirely, I pulled the door after me, and with loose stones, of which there were plenty, so closed it up that no creature could enter. The day was now too far spent to renew the searches of the day before; which I therefore deferred till the next day, when I awoke early, and having provided for my subsistence as before, once more visited these solitary ruins. Meeting nothing new I endeavoured to find my way

---

1   The London edition includes a footnote here referring readers back to page 57.

to the idol; which was not very difficult, as the ruins of the buildings continued quite from my first cell to the idol. As I approached nearer to it, I found the form of the building to vary much from what I had before seen. The rooms or cells here were much larger than the dormitories; and were I suppose the apartments, some of which were still entire, which the priests inhabited. By all that I could see I concluded that this palace had never been raised higher than one story; which might be the reason that it covered so great an extent of ground.

Now, at the distance of about a mile from the place of my abode, as near as I could calculate, I came near to the idol; and here I suppose the temple began; for I found no more apartments, but the remains of a wall, which had antiently, no doubt, surrounded the idol, and left a large area in the middle. In the center stood this idol. Round it was an ascent of twenty stone steps. The image itself, of gold, greatly exceeded human size: it resembled a man clad in a long robe or vest; which reached quite down to the pedestal-stone or foundation on which it stood, and lay in folds upon it. This image was girt about the waist as with a girdle, and on each breast gathered to a point, fastened as it were, with a button; the neck and bosom quite bear[1] like the manner of women; on the head was a curiously wrought crown, and between the two breasts an image of the sun carved in gold, as was all the rest of it. The right hand supported the figure of a new moon, and the left held a cluster of stars. On the back part of the idol was written in large Indian characters to this purpose, THE ORACLE OF THE SUN. I ascended the steps, and threw a stone at the image, and found it was hollow.[2]

Having now pretty well satisfied my curiosity, I began my walk home again. In my way thither, as I kept a strait way as nearly as the buildings would admit, I struck my foot against something and fell down. I got no hurt; as soon as I was up again, I turned round to see at what I had stumbled, and found it to be a large iron bar. Upon removing the earth, that covered

---

1 Bare.

2 Hariot describes a Native American oracle in Appendix B.1.ii.

part of it, I discovered a kind of trapdoor of the same metal, of which this was a part, and two strong bolts. I endeavoured, with stones, to force the bolts open, but did not effect it without great labour, and then with equal difficulty pulled the door up, on the inside of which were two other bolts to fasten it within-side. A stone staircase presented itself; I went down a few steps; but as they led me under the earth, I found it too dark to proceed without a light. But my curiosity was so much excited, that I determined to go home, and fetch a light to explore this subterraneous cavity. For this purpose I brought three shell-lamps and my tinder-box.

As soon as I was got to the bottom of the stairs, and had lost all sight of the light above, I sat down one of my lighted lamps; at a further distance I sat down another in the same maner, and with a third and my tinder-box, in case the light should go out, then proceeded. I made use of these three lights to render the passage less terrifying, and that I might be in less danger of being left in total darkness. I found this passage very narrow, capable of admitting only one person to walk abreast, but high enough to admit a person of more than the highest stature. Almost all the way on each side there were a kind of nitches[1] or holes. Upon examining them I found they contained a variety of things, all of gold, of which I knew not the use, besides a great number of rings, bracelets, lamps, and crowns. An immense treasure! a little further I discovered a kind of room, pretty spacious; in this hung up a great many as I supposed, sacred vestments. These were formed of gold wire, or rather of narrow plated gold curiously folded, or twisted together like net work.

I was surprised to find how little they were tarnished; but the place in which they hung was very dry, and had very little air. Among these vestments were some of more extraordinary workmanship and richness. The largest was, as it were, sprinkled over with precious stones, and here and there a large diamond. It appeared to be in the same fashion with that with which the statue of the sun was clothed. By this hung a kind of

---

1   Niches.

close vest or cassock of the same make, designed I supposed to be worn under the other, with diamond buttons to fasten it. Near this was a crown of most exquisite make, richly beset with precious stones of various sizes and colours; one on the top particularly large, which emitted from all parts of it a light greater than that of my lamp.

In the same room was a golden staff, or rod, with a small image of the sun on the top of it. I supposed these two last vestments might have belonged to the high priest; and the staff likewise. In looking over the gold rings, I found one which was set round with precious stones, with a very large one in the middle, which shone with a lustre equal to that on the top of the crown, as I supposed the high-priests wore; this I put on one of my fingers, and two of the richest bracelets, beset with precious stones, on each of my arms.

Having sufficiently satisfied my curiosity with looking at treasures that could yield me no real service, I walked on a little farther, and found another flight of stairs; these I ascended, wondering whither they would lead me. They were very narrow and steep; which I soon found, led me up into the image of the sun. At last I got quite into the body of it, and my head within the head of it. There were holes through the mouth, eyes, nose, and ears of it; so that I could distinctly see all over the island before me, of which the height I was at gave me a great command. I indeed thought I could even behold the sea.

My astonishment was so great at what I had seen, that I exclaimed aloud, "What wonders are here!" As I spoke these words pretty loud, I had scarcely uttered them, before I was almost stunned with the sound of my own voice. This image, particularly the head of it, it seems, was so wonderfully constructed as to increase the sound of even a low voice to such a degree as to exceed that of the loudest speaker: for afterwards saying, in as low a voice as I could, "What a knowledge of mechanics must the ancients have had!" I might, I dare say, have been heard as far as the human voice is commonly heard intelligibly. Nothing therefore could be more natural for me to conclude than that this image was anciently used to give out oracles: I tried to sing an hymn in my usual pitch of voice; but the sound was too much for my ears to bear; and I was obliged to lower my key.

I now thought it time to descend and go home, lest the night should come on me. The extraordinary things that I had seen afforded me a variety of agreeable reflections in my way home, and took off the horror of the gloominess that the approaching evening shed around me. Nor did the thought of walking among the remains of the dead give me the least terror. Having reached my cell, and prepared to take my rest, I was alarmed with a loud clap of thunder, I cannot say terrified, for I naturally love to hear it thunder; there is something awful and great in it, that always composes my mind, raises it above the things of sense, and fills my mind with noble and exalted ideas of God; whose presence I think it, as it were, bespeaks. I bow and reverence: for though sensible that both it and lightning are the effects of natural causes, yet I consider them as under the direction of God; and doubt not that they are sometimes directed to answer some particular ends of providence.

Storms of this kind, that sometimes happen in Europe, are by no means to be compared to those in these parts; and of the latter sort was that which I am now mentioning. The claps of thunder were prodigious loud and long; the lightning almost without intermission. I was fearful that the stone room I sat in might be thrown down, and therefore went out.

But what did I behold! Imagination can scarcely conceive such a total darkness as then covered the earth; as if every particle of light had been annihilated, and primitive chaos had once more resumed its reign; when in an instant the thunder roared, as if the whole earth had been bursting into atoms, whilst the lightning showed the air one entire body of liquid fire, and so illumined the earth, that I knew not which was brighter, that or the air. It was too much to bear; I again sought my cell, and there trembling waited the dissolution of all things, as I indeed then expected.

I suppose this dreadful hurricane might continue two hours, when it gradually expired, or rather seemed to retire, elsewhere, in more low and distant sounds, and all was calm as though it had always been so. I soon became composed myself, and once more retired to rest. But what a new scene presented itself the next morning, when I came out of my habitation to view the effects that the last night might have produced! My way was frequently obstructed by trees torn up with their roots, and scattered here and there, and the earth in many places covered with the bodies of dead birds, goats, &c. and the carcasses of other small animals, whose names I knew not. But when I approached the sea-shore, the objects were changed; but to such as still showed how dreadful the storm had been. The foam, which the agitated sea had thrown on the shore, lay in great quantities intermixed with a prodigious number of dead fish; some of an enormous size. Many of the rocks were rent in pieces, and their broken fragments made an horrid appearance. What a subject of speculation here for a philosopher!

I now turned my steps back to the more inland parts, where I beheld the same havock made among the trees, beasts, and birds, but no hurt done to the remains of the palace; which I suppose owed its security from the general desolation, to the lowness of it. But I must confess I trembled for the statue of the sun, though I knew not why; for what was it to me whether it stood or fell? As soon as I came near enough, I saw it was safe; and was far from being displeased that it was so.

I now returned home, and having thoroughly gratified my curiosity in searching among the ancient ruins and exploring the contents of them, I spent my time in my little domestic concerns, my devotions, and reading the few books that I found in my chest.

CHAP. IX.

Terrified at the annual visitation of the Indians, she intends to conceal herself in the subterranean passage; resolves to convert the Indians; takes her station in the body of the idol.

THE time now drew pretty near when the Indians were to come to pay their annual visit to the idol of the sun. This reflection put me upon thinking how I should secrete myself during that day. I was indeed informed by the hermit's manuscript, that he contented himself with staying within his cell, and forty years had found that precaution sufficient for his concealment; but still I was afraid to follow his example. Perhaps my being a woman made me more timerous. That, thought I, which has never happened may possibly arrive, and if prudence teaches us always to avail ourselves of the best means in our power, I ought rather to secrete myself in the subterraneous passage, a place in which I shall certainly be less liable to be found; and certainly unused by the hermit, only because unknown to him; for I found no mention of it, and most undoubtedly he would not have passed over, in silence, such an extraordinary discovery. The circumstance of the two bolts within-side of the iron door, which opened into the passage, confirmed my opinion in the fitness of this asylum, as by their means I could fasten myself in.

I had no sooner made my fixed determination to retire to this place, but a very strange thought arose in my mind. It was nothing less than this, to ascend into the hollow idol, speak to the Indians from thence, and endeavour to convert them from their idolatry. A bold attempt! not rashly to be undertaken. I weighed this for several days in my mind. As the manner of my education had afforded me an opportunity of learning several of the Indian dialects, so as to speak them with the utmost ease, I thought it very probable they might speak some one of them; and the construction of the image, as before observed, was such, that if they came within any tolerable distance of it, I should discover whether I understood them or not. If the latter, it would remain only for me to be silent; but if I should understand their language, I thought the extraordinariness of the event, my speaking to them, would appear miraculous, fill them with awe, and prejudice their minds greatly in favour of what I should say to them.[1] I further strengthened my resolution with this reflection, that an attempt to teach the knowledge of the true God to those who know him not, was laudable, and might not want a providential sanction. As to the human means, I knew I was tolerably well principled in the theory of religion, by my uncle's great care, as already mentioned.

With respect to the Indians, I very well knew that they are generally of a docile disposition, and that if you once convince them that your intentions towards them are friendly, no people are more grateful; nor are there any in whom you can, safely, place a greater confidence. Again I considered, that if I should hereafter judge it prudent to discover myself to them, and to go and live among them, that my tawny complexion would be some recommendation. Supposing all this should take place, I thought that though it might not open a way to my return to Europe, yet it might to my living a much happier life, and give me an opportunity of doing abundantly more good, than I had the least reason to think I should ever effect during the whole course of my life. The more I considered the affair, the more resolute I became to undertake it. However, I was determined to give it a very deliberate consideration. Nay, I even made it the subject of my prayers, that if I might become an instrument to promote the knowledge and glory of God, and the salvation and happiness of any of his creatures, I might have his blessing on my endeavours. Surely this was not superstition in one who believes in a particular providence! And of this persuasion shall no man rob me! Certainly he who would divide the belief of a particular providence from religion, destroys that which he should retain. He takes from man that hope which only can support him under the vicissitudes and cares of this life.[2] Let a

---

1 For another account of the use of technology to subdue and convert the Indians, see Appendix B.1.i.
2 Defoe reflects on and defends the concept of providence at considerable length in *Serious Reflections* (187-214).

man be thoroughly persuaded that he is not the subject of divine care, what can support him in the hour of affliction? What can prevent him from seeking relief from the pistol, or the dagger?

But leaving these reflections to those who are so happy as to think, I return to my history. I reflected that as there were several holes, or openings in the image, I might possibly be seen through them by the Indians, before I might have leisure to judge whether I should address myself to them or not; which might be attended with unforeseen consequences, to my great disadvantage. To come to a certainty as to this material point, I proceeded in this manner: I took one of my gowns, and carried it into the statue, and with other things so stuffed it out, as to make it fast within the idol, and to cover all the holes. I then went out upon the island, and carefully surveyed the statue round, and found, to my great satisfaction, that the several perforations grew narrower as they approached the interior part of the statue, and were so deep that they cast a shadow within themselves, so that upon the nearest approach it was impossible to see into it, without there had been a light within-side; however, at least, I could not distinguish my gown; and the statue was too high for any person to bring his eyes, or even his hands, near to the openings. But for fear this deception might be owing to the gown's covering the holes more closely than my body could, I took it away, and once more went out to make a second observation, and had still the pleasure to find it was impossible to see into the statue at all.

Though this danger was entirely removed, there still remained another. I had discovered, as the reader may remember, that such was the wonderful mechanism of this statue, that the least sound became very audible. The noise I might make then at getting into it might instantly discover me; for it was reasonable to suppose, that the visitants would come as near to their idol as they could; no doubt ascend the very steps leading up to it, and being thus near must needs hear the least noise.

Alarming as this consideration was, it soon subsided. For to avoid the possibility of this event, I determined to place myself in it before their arrival, and to sit perfectly still till their departure, if I should see occasion; or till I spoke, if I should find it proper to do so. The image was very well contrived to favour my purpose; there was in it a convenient seat, and sure footing for my feet; and which also luckily suited my stature, so that when I sat, my face was directly upon a level with the holes; by which means I could, without changing my posture, see every thing that was to be seen through them. Looking in my Almanack I found that the night preceding the Thursday on which the Indians were to come, was the time of full-moon; and that, therefore, they, very probably, would take the advantage of it to set out in the night, to be on the island early in the morning. Nor was my conjecture wrong, as the event proved. I thought, therefore, it would be prudent in me to take up my residence early in the evening.

There were now but three days to come before their arrival, during which, I changed my mind, perhaps, as many times as there are hours in that space. This moment I imagined hundreds of Indians prostrate before me with reverence and attention, whilst like a law-giver, I uttered precepts, and, like an orator, inculcated them with a voice magnified almost to the loudness of thunder. At another time my soul shrunk within me at the imagined noise of their dreadful yell; whilst my imagination painted to me an enraged multitude tearing down, in their fury, branches of trees with which to surround the statue, and to burn me in it.

As one, or other of these thoughts prevailed, I resolved for or against, the undertaking. At last, with more than female resolution, I determined on the attempt, and from that moment fortified my mind, and checked every rising fear. This was on the morning of the preceding day of their coming. Out of the few clothes which I had, I chose those which I thought would make the least rustling, and were the least bulky. I thought one shell-lamp would be sufficient, and that I would put that out, when I came to the foot of the statue, as I should take my tinder-box with me. As I intended to get into the statue at night, and knew not how many hours I might be obliged to continue there the next day, I put a few roots into my pocket, and as I had nothing but shells to take any water in with me, and was afraid I might drop them, and make a noise, I contented myself with some ripe limes and other moist fruits, of which there was plenty on the island. When the evening came on, having first performed some particular devotions on the occasion, I set out, and as soon as I had got low enough down the stairs, I fastened the two bolts of the door after me. I should have observed that before I set out, I concealed every thing I had up and down in holes, which I covered up close with stones, so as nothing could be perceived, that in case any of the Indians should chance to wander into my apartments, they should discover nothing that might prompt them to suppose that any human creature inhabited them.

When I came to the foot of the statue I pulled off my shoes, and left them there, that I might not make any noise with them in changing my posture as I sat. Though my situation was dark within, yet as the moon shone very bright, I had a very agreeable prospect of the island. My mind was too busy to suffer me to sleep; the expectation of the events of the coming day engrossed all my thoughts. I hoped, I feared, I trembled, I prayed. For a moment I resolved to descend, and give up the enterprize; again, much courage revived, and I was a heroine. The consciousness of the purity of my intention, and the goodness of my design, prevailed over every other thought, and I became calm and determined. Whilst I thus sat waiting for the arrival of the Indians, and observing the signs of approaching day, a sudden clap of thunder broke just over my head; the introduction to a more violent hurricane than that which I had lately seen. This was accompanied with an earthquake that shook the whole island, and I expected every moment that I should be swallowed up, or, at the best, that the statue would be overturned with myself in it. I now trembled indeed, and all my courage failed. The storm still continuing, I at last, made shift to descend the stairs; and being arrived in the passage, I sat down on the ground, unable to go far into it.

It was darkness all around me, and I could not find my lamp and tinder-box. The earthquake still continued, as I perceived by the motion of the ground beneath me. I thought it could not be long before I should be buried alive in the earth; and therefore, as well as my disturbed spirits would permit, recommended myself into the hands of God.

CHAP. X.

Finds herself unable to get out of the idol; after despairing of extricating herself, forces open the passage; and perceives the earthquake had destroyed her habitation.

In this melancholy situation did I continue for some hours, when I supposed the earthquake was over; for I no longer felt the motion of it. But the thunder still continued, yet with less violence, and the claps were not so frequent. I got up, and once more ascended into the image, saw no appearance of the Indians, and supposed that they would not be able to come at all at that time. Whilst I sat here, I perceived the earth to shake again, and I once more descended into the passage, determined at all events to get out of it, and, if possible, once more, to gain my cell; for I shuddered at the thoughts of being buried alive where I was, which I had but too much reason to fear. I even got over the fear of the Indians coming, and discovering of me, with the hopes that my complexion and the advantage of speaking their language, which I little feared but I should understand, would recommend me to their favour. And with respect to the storm, I might possibly escape without any hurt; and at the worst, I thought it would be better to die by a blast of lightning, or by the stroke of thunder, than to be buried alive in the earth, and very likely be several days in dying.

I should have been glad to have found my lamp; but as I could not, I groped my way as well as I could to the stairs, which led up to the trapdoor, which, having reached, I endeavoured to unbolt; but as the bolts were large and very rusty, they gave me a great deal of trouble and much pain, forced the skin off my hands, and made them very sore and bloody. At last they both gave back, when I pushed the door upwards; but what was my terror at finding it would not give way! I was persuaded that I had unbolted it; and therefore concluded, in my mind, that the earthquake had overturned some of the earth above, and covered it over. It is impossible to describe the agony of my mind; I concluded myself lost, that I was entombed alive, and that I should miserably perish with hunger and thirst. Fear added strength, and I again and again made the utmost efforts to raise the door up, but in vain; I did but increase my pain, and exhaust my strength, till I was unable to make a farther trial.

How dreadful my situation! no other prospect before me but that of a certain lingering death! I sat a long time on the stairs in the most melancholy condition. I endeavoured to pray, but could not; at last I did, when, a little more composed, I got up to look at that light which I never expected to enjoy again with an open freedom. I was satisfied as I crept along, that the earthquake was over. When I was got into the statue, I found that the thunder and lightning still continued. What would I not have given in that moment, to have been exposed to its utmost violence! I most ardently wished for the coming of the Indians, who happily might prove the instruments of my deliverance. But this was rather the wish of despair than a probable event; for how should they know where to find the door, supposing them present and disposed to seek it? Tired with sitting here, or rather with my own tormenting thoughts, I once more, I knew not why, descended into the passage; but what comfort was I to find there? As I got to the bottom of the stairs my foot struck against something, which, upon feeling, I found to be my tinder-box, and by it my lamp. A secret joy spread through my heart. This I instantly checked with this reflection, What comfort, said I to myself, can light afford to such a wretch as I am, doomed to perish in this place? I now upbraided myself with my own folly. Why did I undertake this rash, hazardous enterprize? Could the poor hermit content himself forty years in his lonely cell, and was I so soon weary of it? All the favours of providence are now lost upon me. I might have lived with some degree of comfort, but now must perish miserably. I have by my rashness sinned against the mercy of heaven, and now must die without it.

Thus did I indulge the severest reflections on my own conduct. At last I thought I would once more look at my prison-door, but with no hopes of escape. For this purpose I struck fire, and lighted my lamp, and having reached the door, I carefully examined the bolts, which I thought I discovered to be not quite drawn back; this gave me a little hope. I tried one of them with much pain, for my hands were very sore, and at last it gave back a little; now my hopes were quite revived, and gave me fresh strength to attempt the other, and was again successful, and so happy as to raise the door up. Thus had my mistake procured all this uneasiness to me; and how many of our miseries do often flow from our mistakes? I now once more beheld the open air in freedom, if such can be said of one who was confined in a small island bounded by the sea. I thanked God for my deliverance, and as the day was declining, I intended to make haste to my cell, but found fresh ruins to interrupt my way. Those remains of the palace which I left standing but the day before, were now thrown down; not one had escaped the violence of the earthquake, not even excepting the cell I inhabited. I had reason, indeed, to be very thankful for my confinement in the subterraneous passage, to which, in all probability, I owed my not having perished in my cell. But one misfortune I still sustained, the want of an apartment above ground.

The thoughts of living under-ground were very disagreeable; but no better habitation remained for me. It was well for me, that I had the precaution to remove my few effects out of my cell, which by the fall of it might have been destroyed, but which I found safe where I had deposited them. I took some provisions, and some more lamps and fat, in order to render my dark abode as light as I could, and with an heavy heart returned back to the place I had left but a little while before, not thinking I should ever have made it the voluntary place of my residence, if indeed I may say voluntary; for it was a necessity, not a free choice, that led me thither. Having entered by the door and fastened it, I lighted five other lamps, with that I carried in my hand ready lighted, but these were not sufficient to take off the gloominess of the place. I had no better lodging than the bare ground; for it was too late to furnish myself with leaves.

A melancholy situation this! and scarcely was I able to bear it; but I summoned every thing that could give me comfort, or inspire me with fortitude. Among other things I considered that it was in every respect better than being on the ground above, exposed to the air and other accidents; that here, at least, was a safe retreat; that my distress was neither owing to my own sin or folly; and that, above all, no place is excluded from the presence of God; that his providential eye was still watching over me, and that I was under his protection. Having taken some refreshment, which I greatly needed, and said my prayers, I laid me down in one of the apartments here, already mentioned, with all my lamps burning, and, being tolerably composed in my mind, and very weary and heavy, having had no rest the night before, I fell fast asleep.

CHAP. XI.

The Indians land, and approach the idol; the high-priest interrogates the statue, from which she makes responses, and instructs them in the principles of the Christian religion.

As soon as I awoke I got up, and finding one of my lamps yet burning, I took one of them, walked to the stairs that led up to the statue, which I ascended, and found the sun had been risen for some time, and that it was a very fine calm morning. I had not been here long before I heard a prodigious noise of voices, when looking forwards, I discovered a great number of Indians approaching, at some distance. The noise and sight of them startled me at first; but recovering myself from the surprize, my former intention of speaking to them revived, and I was the more confirmed in my resolution to do so from a consideration of the almost impossibility of living long under ground. Therefore first commending myself to God, and my intention, I waited for a favourable opportunity; in the mean time sitting as still as possible.

There was a great number of them, men, women, and children, who as they drew nearer formed themselves, as it were, into ranks, the oldest men first, then the younger, after these the eldest women, and the youngest; lastly the children, (no infants) boys and girls, the last of which brought up the rear. But I should have observed that the whole body of them was preceded by six old men, their priests, with a very old man at their head, so feeble with age that he was supported by two others. As soon as they had formed themselves in this manner, they came on very slowly, and with a profound silence. This slow march greatly favoured me, and gave me time to be thoroughly composed and fortified. I supposed their reasons were partly reverence, and partly to favour their ancient feeble high-priest; for such he was to the sun. Each of the priests had a small golden image suspended at his breast, and a golden coronet. The high priest the same, only that his coronet was much larger; he had besides a long staff in his right hand, with an image of the sun upon the top of it, also of gold.

Having approached within a few yards of the statue, they all stopt; when the high priest, and the six others, with the whole assembly, very devoutly prostrated themselves to the earth three times: all of them continued prostrate on the ground, except the six priests who each kneeled on both his knees, whilst the high-priest kneeled only upon one. The high priest then begun to sing a kind of hymn, in praise of the sun, as God, joined soon after by the priests, and, lastly, as in a chorus, by the whole assembly. The sound of their voices was so increased by the make of the statue, that I was hardly able to bear it.

I still kept silence; not thinking it as yet a proper time to interrupt them. When this part of their worship was over, they all stood, and the high-priest made an address to the sun, in a very low feeble voice, which yet I could hear very plainly, and to my great joy and encouragement, perfectly understood. The purport of it was to acknowledge him as the author of all things, the support of all, and the giver of all things, with praises naturally resulting from such acknowledgments. Then each of the priests, in his turn, offered up a kind of prayer for long life, health, success in hunting and fishing, &c. The address of the high-priest was truly great and elevated, and a pleasing simplicity and a fervency of devotion ran through the prayers of the priests, which they delivered very distinctly and audibly. When the priests had finished their parts, the whole assembly, which had hitherto observed a profound silence, except in the chorus, begun theirs. A confused disharmonious noise ensued; for each had a petition to offer up, whilst like the priests of Baal, they cried as loud as they could, as if their God was a great way off, or deaf, and could not hear them. In these supplications even the children bore a part.

And now the high-priest begun again, but in a different manner than before, who stood, as did the rest, and very pathetically lamented the long silence of the oracle, and, in a kind of agony, intreated that answers might be again given to them. He ceased at times, when each of the other priests, in his turn, continued the same complaint, and the same intreaties. Every time that one of the priests stopped, the whole company made great lamentations, attended with the most dreadful yells.

The seven priests having finished this last part, a general and profound silence ensued.

I now was preparing to speak, thinking I could not have a better opportunity, when the high-priest gave me a much fairer occasion; for, raising his voice, seemingly, as loud as he could, he cried, or asked, in a kind of exultation,

WHO IS GOD BUT THE SUN?

To whom I immediately replied, in so very loud, yet equally distinct, a voice, that it ecchoed back again from the end of the island,

HE WHO MADE THE SUN.

I must acknowledge I trembled when I had done, and was even sorry I had spoken, though truly and properly; yet I rightly concluded that I must proceed – No sooner had I uttered these words, but the lay-assembly leaped up from the ground, as if frantick with joy, and with loud shouts, and strange gestures, expressed the transports they felt, and then all fell prostrate, whilst the priests, with more decency and gravity, profoundly bowed their bodies, three times, to the very earth.

And now the following dialogue commenced between the high-priest and me, the people observing the whole time a solemn silence.

High-Priest. "Who then is that God?"

Answer. "He who always was, is, and ever will be."

High-Priest. "Where does he dwell?"

Answer. "In heaven, though indeed he is present every where; for he filleth heaven and earth with his presence – He sees all things; knows all things; for he made all things, and supports all things, by his power, which is boundless."

High-Priest. "Can we see him?"

Answer. "No; for no man can see God whilst he lives."

High-Priest. "Shall we then see him after we are dead?"

Answer. "Yes; all good men shall see him, and be happy with him; but every wicked man will be banished from his presence, and be miserable."

High-Priest. "Who is a good man?"

Answer. "He who believes in God, who loves and obeys him, and does by every man as he would be done by."

High-Priest. "Who is a wicked man?"

Answer. "He who does not believe in God, love, and obey him; and he who does not do by every one as he would be done by."

Here after a short silence, he continued his questions.

High-Priest. "Are you God?"

Answer. "No."

High-Priest. "Are you the sun?"

Answer. "No; for the sun can neither understand, nor see, nor hear, as I do."

High-Priest. "Who are you then?"

Though I did not mean to impose myself upon them as God, and had declared I was not God, yet I thought it necessary to check this question, judging it as yet too soon to declare myself, and therefore replied,

Answer. "Do not ask; for I will not answer to any questions but as I see proper."[1]

At this instant our dialogue was strangely stopt, and I was greatly surprized to see the whole assembly throw themselves upon the ground, tear, and beat themselves, venting their grief in cries and unintelligible accents, the priests behaving as madly as they. Whilst I beheld this extraordinary change with a concern and surprize that prevented my speaking to them, they all ran away, except the high-priest, who was too feeble, as fast as they could towards the sea-side.

For my own part my ideas were so confused upon this occasion, that I was incapable of thought. What have I said, at last cried I, within myself, that could thus terrify these people? I paused, and as my custom is on all sudden and extraordinary events, endeavoured to withdraw my attention from all outward things, and recollect my mind within me; and now happily I guessed the cause, as the event proved. I had told them I was neither the God I had described, nor the sun, whom they believed to be God, and yet refused to inform them who I was; yet I must have appeared to them to be more than a mere mortal, and recollecting that it was an opinion, common among the

---

1 Other uses of the dialogue form for conversion efforts include works by John Eliot and Thomas Wilson.

untaught Indians, to believe that there are two beings, the one good and the other evil, answering to God and the Devil with us Christians, therefore, from their sudden strange behaviour, I concluded, that they apprehended I must be the latter, the evil being whom they dreaded, and therefore fled.[1] This determined the conduct I was to pursue. I therefore immediately called to the high-priest, who lay on the ground, "Arise, and learn to be wise and happy."

But observing that he continued motionless, and not knowing but he might be dead, I extended my voice to the highest pitch I could, depending on the mechanism of the statue, for its reaching to the ears of the affrighted multitude; and thus called after them: "Return, I am not the evil being whom ye dread; return and provoke me not, to destroy you, before you can reach your own shore."

I know not whether the casuists may justify this artifice from sin; but to me it appeared expedient, and was successfully adapted to their fears, for they immediately halted, and began slowly to return back. At this instant, perceiving the high-priest to move, I repractised the same artifice on him. "Arise," said I, "and I will neither destroy you, nor the people; but if you would procure my favour, encourage them to return, and to attend to my instructions."

He immediately arose; and turning to the people, beckoned to them to come forwards. This encouraged them to come again to their former station; when he said to them, "The oracle will not hurt you; but he will be heard."

This was as I wished; but, observing the signs of fear still strongly stampt upon them, I thus addressed them:

"Fear not, I am not the evil being; and if you will hearken to me, he shall never hurt you."

These words had the desired effect; they immediately appeared calm and pleased, bowing to the earth with profound reverence. After this the high-priest spoke to me, with a trembling voice.

---

1 For early English accounts of religious practice among the southern Algonquian see Appendix B.1.i and B.3.ii. Defoe's views of North American native religion and his attitude toward conversion are expressed in Appendix A.2.vii.

High-Priest. "Will you protect us from the evil being, that he may not hurt us?"

Answer. "God, who hath all power only, and who is good and gracious, will protect you, and will not suffer the evil being to hurt you."

High-Priest. "But must we not pray to the evil being not to hurt us?"

Answer. "No; you must pray to God only."

High-Priest. "Must we not pray to the Sun?"

Answer. "No; for he was made by God, to give you light and heat, and has no understanding."

High-Priest. "Will he not be angry then, and leave us in the dark."

Answer. "No; look at that tree on your right hand, you know it grows, bears leaves and fruit; do you think it can see, or hear, or understand?"

High-Priest. "I don't know."

Answer. "Can it move about from place to place, as you do?"

High-Priest. "I believe not?"

Answer. "I told you before that God made all things; the sun is one of those things which he hath made by his great power, and hath fixed it in the air, but it cannot move from place to place, by any power that it hath in itself, as you can, but is moved as God pleases. It can neither see, hear, speak, nor think as you can, who therefore art a more excellent creature than the sun, and therefore must not worship him, for he was made for your use, any more than you should worship that tree, because it does you good by bearing fruit for you to eat: nor must you worship any other creature you see, for the same reason; because they are all made by God for your use, and he hath given them to you."

High-Priest. "Did God send you to teach us?"

Answer. "He brought me hear,[1] and I will teach you."

As it was now high noon, I thought they might want to refresh themselves, and therefore said, "You may now eat and drink, and then I will speak to you again." The whole assembly

---

1   Here.

then bowed themselves, with great reverence, three times to the ground, and then sat down to eat and drink.

I was myself very glad to have a little time, to consider how I should proceed on this extraordinary occasion. Whilst I took some refreshment myself, I reflected very deliberately upon this important business I had undertaken, and prayed to God that I might be the means of instructing them in the truth, and bring them, happily, to the knowledge of Christianity. But as this affair required a very mature deliberation, I thought it would be best to dismiss them at this time, and order some of them to come again the next week. As soon then as I found that they had finished their repast, I said to the high-priest, "I would have you now, all of you, return home, and you the priests, and as many of you as will, may come here again this day week, but not before, upon pain of my displeasure, and then I will instruct you further."

Upon this they all set up a shout of joy, and having made their obeisances as before, returned back to the shore, in a reversed order from that they came in; for now the children walked first, the grown people next, and the priests last, carrying the high-priest with them.

End of VOL. I.[1]

---

1 The London edition contains a notice, printed between the first and second volumes of the text, issued by some proprietors of circulating libraries which explains that subscription rates for lending books will be increased. The note, titled "Reputable Circulating Libraries," is dated November 8, 1766.

VOLUME TWO

CHAP. I.

Our heroine traverses the island; description of an uncommon animal, with her thoughts thereon.

I HAD matter enough to employ my thought during this interim, to reconsider what I had said, and what method I should pursue for the future with these people. Besides, I had some domestick cares upon my hands: I now set about preparing a better convenience for my rest by night, and busied myself the remainder of the day, as soon as I perceived the people were gone off the island, with gathering leaves and other things to make my bed, which at last I made pretty tolerable. The next day I removed all the things I had concealed into the subterraneous apartments, bestowing some in one and some in another. I found it necessary also to provide myself with more fat, that I might now want light, and indeed with some meat; for these purposes I was obliged to kill a couple of goats, a task always disagreeable to me. As my habitation was very gloomy and melancholy, I spent what leisure time I had; in walking up and down the island. In these few days, I saw more of it than I had in all the time I had been upon the island. I found it well watered with little rivulets, and vast variety of trees, many of which bore different kinds of fruits. Those which I perceived had been pecked by birds I tasted, and found some of them very delicious.

Among the various kinds of birds I found one sort exceeding beautiful. It was about the size of a large parrot; its feathers delightfully variegated with the colours of the rain-bow, those of its tail spreading like those of the peacock; but not near so large, nor numerous. Of the four-footed animals I saw one of a most extraordinary kind. It was of the size of a large dog, as to its body, but its legs, which were very long, were by no means proportioned to the bulk of this strange animal, being so slender as to bend under him, insomuch that it could move only with the utmost slowness. I wondered within myself how this creature could either defend, or provide for itself; but observing it more closely, I took notice that its eyes were uncommonly large, for an animal of that size, projecting far from the head, and so frightful as to excite fear in me; and I should have fled from it, only that I perceived it could not overtake me, had I walked ever so slow. The mouth of it was no less dreadful; it kept the lips of it almost constantly drawn asunder, which showed two horrid rows of sharp, but short teeth.

It was at this time labouring to get into a kind of pasture. I determined to watch its motions, thinking it might be seeking its prey; for I did not doubt but that the goodness and wisdom of providence, which had thus wonderfully provided for its security, had doubtless taken no less care for its support. It was a long time in getting to the place it seemed designed to reach. As it walked or rather limped along, several animals passed it, many much bigger than itself, who no sooner saw it than they ran from it, as if afraid of being destroyed by it. I took notice that as any of these approached him, he rowled[1] his eyes, which encreased their fierceness, at the same time showing his teeth.

At length he got into the grass, and then laid himself down, extended as if dead. I came up to him behind, for his looks were too terrifying to face him, and sitting down at some distance, was resolved to watch, that I might discover whether he chose this place merely for rest, or with some other view. He soon changed his posture a little, so that I could perceive that his eyes were shut, and his lips closed; I therefore concluded that he was going to sleep; however, I still continued in my place. The hair on his body was very thick and long, perhaps five or six inches; the extremities of every cluster of them formed a kind of bunch, or small tuft, as large as an hasel-nut. Having sat about a quarter of an hour, I saw a great number of field-mice come up to him, who presently began to nibble at these tufts, the animal continuing to lie still; but after a very considerable number of mice had thus employed themselves, he got up, and shook himself violently, when, to my great astonishment, I found these mice, some way or other so fastened and secured to these tufts, that very few of them could disengage themselves. And now, his neck being very long, he turned his

1 Rolled.

head, and devoured them very greedily, one after another. I dare say that in a few minutes, he ate near three hundred of them; for his body was almost covered with them.

My curiosity was amply gratified, if an human being may say so, of the sudden destruction of such a number of innocent animals; but the divine being has been pleased to permit animals to support themselves by devouring one another. I say permit; for I cannot think that it was the original design of the Almighty, that animals should at all destroy one another. I suppose it rather to be one of the unhappy consequences of the general corruption of nature. I know it may be replied, that some animals seem by their make to be designed to subsist on animal food only, and are accordingly provided with teeth and claws, unadapted for feeding on herbage, or fruits, and with stomachs evidently made for digesting animal substances; whilst those parts in animals who eat no animal food, are quite differently formed. I know and grant this; but yet my opinion is not by this concession destroyed. For it is highly reasonable to suppose, that these kind of creatures were so formed to prey upon dead animals, that by their feeding upon them, they might remove what would otherwise be an hurtful nuisance, in more senses than one. However, it is not my intention, here, to display the naturalist; otherwise I think, though a woman, I should gain the laurel from an Aristotle or a Pliny, were they to oppose me on this subject.[1]

But to return to the event which gave rise to this digression, I should be very glad if I could inform the reader, and especially myself, by what means these mice were entangled by, or fastened to, the tufts of hair, so as not be enabled to disengage themselves, no not even when the creature shook himself so violently, which, one would naturally think, was a circumstance in their favour. However, since I am upon this subject, which at least is pleasing to myself, and I think no ignoble contemplation for an ingenuous mind, I will hazard my own conjecture

---

[1] Among his other works, the Greek philosopher Aristotle wrote several biological treatises, including *The History of Animals, On the Parts of Animals, On the Progression of Animals*, and *On the Generation of Animals*. Pliny, a Roman naturalist, wrote *Historia Naturalis*. For the ancients, laurel symbolized victory and merit.

upon the occasion. As we know, by the assistance of the microscope, that the hairs of animals are pervious, or hollow, and that they are pervaded by some kind of liquid matter, for their growth and nourishment, perhaps that with which the hairs of this animal are filled and nourished may be of a more extraordinary glutinous kind, and as the tufts formed by the extremities of these hairs are pretty big, a large quantity of this glutinous matter being lodged there, the nibbling of the mice breaking the hairs, this glutinous matter may so fasten the hairs to the inside of their mouths, as to render it exceeding difficult for them to disengage themselves, at least soon enough to prevent their being devoured: and I think the shaking of the animal must doubly contribute to their danger; because this motion prevents them from fixing their feet against his body, which would assist them in disengaging their mouths from the tufts, and being thus in a hanging state, their fear may make them bite the tufts the closer, upon the motion of the beast, and thereby render them a still easier victim: so that nature seems to have endowed him with this artifice the more effectually to secure his prey.[1]

---

1   Descriptions of unusual flora and fauna, or rarities, characterize New World travel narratives as early as Columbus.

CHAP. II.

The Indians return to the island; she continues her instructions, and commands them to return weekly.

THUS did I busy or amuse myself; and indeed I cannot imagine to myself any situation in which a thinking being, free from pain of body, and great anxiety of mind, cannot divert itself. I can always find something, from without or within myself, for my amusement. Often have I been diverted with watching the flights of a fly, or the excursions of a spider, till my mind has been so filled with the display of the infinite wisdom of the Creator, in the formation of his works, as to elevate my mind to the most exalted adoration. Nor does darkness deprive me of my mental amusements: in this state I can reflect on those things that I have seen, heard, or read of. The recollection of these sets my busy imagination at work, and I am pleased, nay, I am happy; and darkness has no horrors for me.

How miserable must those be who complain for want of amusement! How wretched such a state! What! want matter for thought? Can a thinking being, such as man is, say thus? Look round, is not all nature about thee teeming with subjects well adapted for thy contemplation, happily prepared for thy entertainment? But whither will my thoughts carry me? my province is not that of a philosopher, but historian. And if my reader has travelled thus far with me, I doubt not but he is impatient to hear again of my late visitors, perhaps more so than I was. Nor do I wonder that events so extraordinary should attract his attention; and if ever they should be published in any country, I doubt not but they will soon be naturalized throughout Europe, and in different languages, and in succeeding ages, be the delight of the ingenious and inquisitive; and that some future bold adventurer's imagination, lighted up by my torch, will form a fictitious story of one of his own sex, the solitary inhabitant of a desolate island.[1] Such imaginary

---

1   "Our authoress here seems to please herself, with the thoughts of the immortality of her history, and to prophesy of that of Robinson Crusoe, which only is inferior to her own, as fiction is to truth." – *Author's / "Editor's" note.*

scenes, like those of a play, may have a temporary effect, but not permanent, like the real ones of mine.[1]

At length the appointed morning came, against whose advent I took care to be ready placed within the statue. Having waited a short time, I saw only the seven priests advancing towards me. I wondered not to see them followed by any of their people, and thought it very odd. When they were come up pretty near, they stopt, and having made their accustomed obeisances, stood silent, I supposed waiting till I spoke. After I had reflected a little on this occasion, I begun. "Why has none of the people attended you?"

High-Priest. "It is our business to instruct the people, and if you will please to teach us, we will inform them accordingly."

Answer. "Why?"

High-priest. "Because we live by teaching them, and if you only should teach them, they will not give us those good things which they now do."

Answer. "But I will not teach you only; I will teach them also. Nor need you fear losing your subsistence. I will take care it shall be continued. Hear me then, and if you fear me, observe my command. Let one of you go and fetch some of the people; and let the rest of the priests wait here till the others return."

The peremptory manner in which I uttered these words, seemed to affect them much. They made their usual obeisances; and then the high-priest answered, "that they were very ready to comply with my commands; but that it would rather take up too much time, to go back to their countrymen, and return again the same day, to make any convenient stay afterwards, to hear my instructions; but that if I pleased they would return home, and attend me, with some of the people, in the morning."

To this I agreed, and accordingly they immediately withdrew, having taken a respectful leave.

As soon as they were gone, I descended into my subterrane-

---

1 In an apparent attempt to deflect anticipated criticisms that this novel is an imitation of Defoe's *Crusoe*, the author has the narrator Unca Eliza Winkfield retroactively accuse Defoe of imitation; Winkfield boldly "predicts" that her story will be adopted, fictionalized, and masculinized by a "later" writer.

ous apartments, took some refreshments, and spent the remainder of the day in providing some necessaries, and rambling
about the island. The next morning, I took care early to place
myself in the statue. Nor had I waited very long, before I perceived the priests coming forward, with a considerable number
of the people with them. The usual ceremonies past, I began to
discourse upon the nature and attributes of the Deity, from
what are usually called the principles of natural religion;
though I believe, strictly speaking, all religion to be revealed.[1]
I stopt at every convenient pause, two or three minutes, that I
might not weary their attention, and give them opportunity to
reflect, as it were step by step, upon what I said.

As I was well acquainted with the manners of the Indians, I
adapted my discourse to their own way of reasoning, and
avoided all such terms, and modes of speech, as are intelligible
only to Europeans. When I had discoursed near three hours in
this manner, I desisted, desiring them to take some refreshment,
with which I saw they had provided themselves, and that afterwards I would call to them; and then the priests, or any of the
people, might ask what questions they should please concerning what I had delivered. I ordered them to retire to some
distance from where they were. This I did, that I might not
be heard, as I intended to withdraw for a little time out of the
statue, to take some refreshment myself.

As soon as I had taken my place as before, I called to my
audience, who respectfully returned to their former station. I
repeated the leave I had given them, to ask any questions rela-
tive to my discourse. All the priests, in their turns, asked me
several pertinent and sensible questions; to which I replied as
well as I was able and I believe to their satisfaction. But observing that the laity still kept silence, I endeavoured to encourage
them to propose their questions also, and was answered, by
some, "We know nothing; our priests know all; teach our

---

1   By beginning her instruction with natural religion, Winkfield appears to be follow-
    ing the program set out by the Society for the Propagation of the Gospel in For-
    eign Parts (SPG) for converting Indians (see, for example, *A Collection of Papers*, ix).
    The SPG, founded in 1701, was dedicated to advancing the Church of England
    abroad through missionary work. Defoe discusses natural and revealed religion in
    Serious Reflections (186-87).

priests, and they will teach us." From this I concluded, that the priests had dealt in private with them, and had forbid their asking any questions, that they might preserve their superiority among them.[1]

I therefore addressed myself to them with some sharpness, reminding them of what I had told them before, "that I would not teach them only, but that I would teach the people also."

Upon this the priests submissively bowed, and declared their readiness to obey my commands. I then proceeded, as well as I could, further to explain what I had delivered in the fore part of the day; and concluded with telling them, I should be ready to continue my instructions to them, for that I had much more to say, once a week, provided the priests would attend that day week, and so on, with as many of the people as should choose to come; but as the high-priest was very aged and infirm, he might come, or not, as he pleased. To this the high-priest said he would conform. I then told them they might return home as soon as they pleased; and it was not long before they all quitted the island.

---

1   Crusoe's religious instruction to Friday likewise includes warnings against "priest-craft." See Appendix A.2.iii.

CHAP. III.

Perplexed in what manner to act, she ascends the idol, addresses the Indians, and informs them, that a person shall come to instruct them in the knowledge of the true God.

I now once more found myself left to my little occupations, and to my own thoughts. I soon, and easily, fulfilled the demands of the former; but not so those of the latter. I had engaged in an affair that required the utmost attention, and not the smallest abilities. This latter reflection startled me. What an arduous attempt? thought I, and was abashed; would I had never engaged! but how can I desist? This was as difficult to answer, as how to go on. As I knew something of the manner of the Indians, I did not doubt of their docibility;[1] but I was very suspicious of the priests. I foresaw they would never easily suffer themselves to become useless to the people, and nothing less could be the consequence of my instructing them. And supposing this to be got over, how was I to proceed to continue teaching them from the statue, if I hoped to make any tolerable progress, as it would render their attendance more frequent than might be convenient to them? and in the wet season they could not come at all; and further, how could I, with any possible degree of comfort, continue to live under ground even in the summer? and in the winter I should be entirely confined under ground. This last thought affected me so much, that I saw the absolute necessity of going to live among the Indians, whatever my success in teaching, or reception, might prove. I determined to trust in providence for a discharge of the first; and no less to rely on its protection, as to my personal security. Though I had thus determined the part I was to take, there yet remained a great difficulty, how to introduce myself among them. They might at present conceive of me as more than mortal, reverence me, and pay an implicit faith to all my teachings; but how would their opinion of me change, when they should discover me to be a mere mortal, a destitute stranger,

---

1 Docility.

even needing their support! What credentials had I to support the novel doctrines that I was to introduce? How was I to combat old opinions, handed down from father to son, received with reverence, and, no doubt, maintained with obstinacy? What advantage would not all these difficulties give the priests over me, among an ignorant and deluded people? and what might not exasperated bigotry prompt them to? nay, I knew not, but they might even think it necessary and right to destroy one who should dare to deny the deity of the sun, and expose the absurdity of their religion.

These were discouraging reflections, and the more I considered them, the more I was intimidated; and I heartily repented that I had ever spoken to them, and again was irresolute as to going among them. Thus was I distracted whether I determined to stay, or go; to stay was attended with certain evils, to go, too probably, with very great ones. Miserable wretch! cried I, what shall I do? tears succeeded; and I could think no more, with any coherence. As soon as I was a little composed, I had recourse to my usual consolation, prayer; and now my mind was calm, I could view the difficulties before me without terror, and distinguish between positive and real dangers.

I concluded to trust providence, in adopting that course, which, upon the most mature consideration, should appear to have the fewest difficulties, and the most advantages on its side. It was to go among the Indians; the manner thus; not to acquaint them in the least with my condition, that they might not conceive any prejudices against me on that account, and that by keeping them ignorant who I was, or how I came to them, I might preserve a superiority over them, sufficient to keep them in awe, and to excite their obedience: yet I determined to speak no untruth. Accordingly, when the day of their return arrived, and the priests, and a great many of the people were present before the statue, I thus addressed them:

Oracle. "Be attentive, and hear! You are a people ignorant of the knowledge of the true and only God, who made heaven and earth, and every thing therein; you are also ignorant of that worship, which God expects from his creatures; and of that happiness, which he will bestow upon all those who worship him according to his holy will.

"This his holy will he hath revealed to many thousands of men and women like you, who live in other parts of the earth, and now you also may know his holy will and be happy.

"God hath been pleased to send into the world, from time to time, holy men, and sometimes women, to instruct mankind in the knowledge of him; and at last his son, to instruct them more fully.

"But forasmuch as mankind had by their great wickedness offended God, of whom you are a part, he would have punished them with a very grievous punishment; but his son, who loved them, came down upon earth and was made a man, and offered himself up a sacrifice to his father, that mankind might be forgiven, reconciled unto his father, and be made good people, by believing and doing as he taught them.

"He was, whilst upon earth, attended by certain persons, called his disciples, who wrote the history of his life. This history, with the writings of the holy men, who lived before his coming into the world, and the writings of his disciples, designed to teach all men, you shall have for your instruction.

"With respect to teaching you the holy religion of the son of God from this place, it will be too inconvenient to you to come here as often as necessary; and during the rainy seasons, every year, it will be impossible for you to come at all.

"Therefore, that you may not want that instruction, which is necessary to your happiness here, and after you are dead, you shall be taught in this manner.

"A person shall come to you, like yourselves, and that you may be the less fearful or suspicious, that person shall be a woman, who shall live among you as you do.

"She shall bring with her the holy writings I have been speaking of, and shall teach all of you, especially your priests, who shall instruct you after her departure, the knowledge of the true God, and the way to be happy for ever.

"You must be sure to show the greatest respect to her, do every thing that she shall command you, never ask who she is, from whence she comes, or when, or whether she will leave you. Never hinder her from coming to this island when she pleases, nor follow her hither without her leave. You must all believe, and do as she shall instruct you, and never presume to come to this island without her leave, or do any thing that she forbids.

"But I do not want to force her among you: if you do not choose she should come, speak, and she shall not come; and I will be dumb for ever."

Answer. "Let her come! let her come! let her come! and we will love and obey her."[1]

This was the cry of all, with a noise in my ears like that of thunder; whilst they showed every outward sign of joy. As soon as all were again silent, I once more addressed them.

Oracle. "Hear me then, let as many of you as please come here three days hence, two hours after the sun is risen, and you will see her sitting upon these steps, drest like the high-priest of the sun. Receive her with great respect, and conduct her to your country, and remember all I have said."

I now was silent, when the whole multitude shouted,

Answer. "We will meet her! we will meet her!"

This important business of the day being thus concluded, they all returned home, and left me not a little pleased at the happy expedient I had devised to procure myself a favourable retreat among the Indians, and a high probability of success in my future teachings.

It now only remained to prepare for my departure. The day before the return of the Indians I collected together all my clothes, and the few books that I had; but had no chest to put them in, having broken that when I tumbled it down from the rock. I considered how to supply this want, and at last concluded to tie them up as well as I could with twigs, having no cords. Having first chosen such things as I intended to make my appearance in, I wrapt my bundle up in one of the priest's golden vestments, and put in two others. The last evening I spent in particular prayers upon the ensuing occasion.

---

1 This cry calls to mind the original seal of the Massachusetts Bay Colony, which represents an Indian who, echoing the Macedonian's appeal to Paul in Acts 16:9, cries "Come over and help us."

CHAP. IV.

Apparels herself in the richest manner, and waits the approach of the Indians; acquaints them she was sent by the oracle; presents them with rings, and partakes of a repast.

WHEN the expected morning came, I awoke by day-break, drest myself in white, and, over all, put on the high-priest's vestments, that I had found upon my first searching of the subterraneous apartments. These were a kind of cassock, or vest, formed of gold wire, or rather of small narrow plated gold, curiously folded, or twisted together, like net-work, which buttoned close with diamonds. Over this I put on, formed of the same materials, and in the same manner, a gown, sprinkled all over with precious stones, and here and there a large diamond. On my head I placed a crown of most exquisite make, richly beset with precious stones of various sizes and colours; one on the top particularly large, which emitted from all parts of it a light greater than that of either of my lamps. In my right hand I held a golden staff, or rod, with a small image of the sun on the top of it. On one of my fingers I wore the ring, and on each arm a rich bracelet, all which I found at the same time I discovered all these other things.

I had made myself a kind of wicker basket, which I filled with a great number of gold rings, all from the same repository. When I first discovered all these treasures, I then little thought they would ever prove of any real use to me. Nor did I now thus adorn myself from pride; but I thought the extraordinary appearance that they would give me, might procure me a more favourable reception. The rings I designed for presents. I should have mentioned that, besides the fine ring that I put on, when first I found the rings, I put one upon each of my fingers.

When I left my subterraneous dwelling, I not only bolted the door, but covered it over with earth. Being come to the statue I sat down on the biggest step, in all my finery, the crown on my head, my staff in my right hand, and on my left stood my twig-basket; at some distance lay my bundle, which, being wrapt up in one of the gold vestments, glittered, as the sun shone very bright.

Thus I sat, with my bow and arrows hung over my shoulders, waiting for the important interview, my mind not a little agitated between hope and fear. However, I very solemnly recommended myself and my undertaking to God; and then endeavoured to fortify my mind so that on the approach of the Indians I might not discover the least symptom of fear; for I knew on this much depended.

I had sat near an hour before they approached; but at last saw them advance in the same order as at their first coming. At the first sight of them my heart leapt, and every limb trembled, and for a moment I wished myself within my subterraneous habitation. But as they advanced slowly, I had time enough to recover myself, and, before they came near enough to distinguish my countenance, I believe it was sufficiently steady.

As they came near, led by the high-priest and the others, they bowed almost to the ground at every step; I still kept my seat looking firmly at them. When they were come near enough to hold a conversation, they halted, and the priests and all the company, who were about two hundred, without any children, prostrated themselves to the ground; I then arose, and extending my golden rod towards them said, "Arise."

They did so; when, observing that they held a profound silence, I thus addressed them, with as much affability as I could; yet with an air of superiority.

"I suppose you are come to invite me to reside in your country?"

To this the high-priest answered, "Yes;" which was presently ecchoed throughout the whole multitude.

I then desired the high-priest to sit down at my right hand, which he did, not without some mannerly reluctance; I then placed the other priests on the steps a little lower on the right and left hand.

Sitting with the priests in this manner, I again addressed them:

"I suppose most of you were here three days ago, and heard, or know, what was then delivered from above," pointing up to the statue. "In consequence of what was then promised you, and to which you who were then present agreed, I am come to live among you, at least for some time, and to instruct you; observe what was then enjoined you.

"You must obey my commands, observe my instructions, never ask who I am, from whence I come, or whether, or when, I will leave you.

"Though if at any time you should desire me to quit your country, you may tell me so, and I will leave you. And further, you are never to oppose my coming here, as I shall do from time to time, nor any of you presume to follow me hither.

"If you will faithfully observe these things, I will come and live with you, acquaint you with the holy books of God, instruct you in the knowledge of God, and in the ways of his religion; which will make you happy for ever."

Here I paused; when the high-priest arose up with great reverence, and having bowed three times, almost to the ground, said, "Holy woman, we heard, with great attention what the oracle said, and when we returned into our country we called, the next day, all our countrymen together, and told them every thing that the oracle had delivered. Our countrymen rejoiced to hear the good news, and all desire you will come and live among them; they will love you, obey all your commands, and will make you their queen, for our king is lately dead, and as he had no children, we have not as yet chosen a new king. Will you therefore go home with us, and be our queen?"

Answer. "I thank you for your kind offer; but I will not be your queen, therefore you may choose whom you please. But, as you desire it, I will come and live among you, and will be only your instructor."

I had scarcely finished my answer, before the whole company made the greatest acclamations of joy, crying out,

"Come! Come! Come! and make us happy."

I arose up, and, after their manner, made three respectful bows to them; which were returned with new acclamations of joy.

As soon as all were silent again, I sat down, and taking out of my twig-basket two of the best rings, I presented them to the high-priest, and to each of the priests two others, near in goodness to those of the high-priest's; when, finding that I had a sufficient number of rings, I desired the people to come to me one by one, and I presented each with a ring, which they all received with great expressions of joy.

I soon found that they were confounded in their ideas about me, and conceived of me, as one more than mortal; for the high-priest, with great reverence, asked me if I ever ate and drank?

I chearfully replied "Yes; and if you have brought any provisions, I will eat and drink with you." At this he seemed both pleased and surprised. He then called to some of the people, who came forwards, bringing a kind of wicker baskets. The contents of them were dried fish, goats flesh, and other animal food, various kinds of fruit, dried corn, and a liquor like wine.

Before I began to eat, I stood up and said grace, at which they seemed much surprised. Then the priests and I took a comfortable repast together; whilst the people sat down, and did the same, we all observing a profound silence during the whole time. When we had finished, I again surprised them with returning thanks, according to the manner of christians.

The high-priest, hearing me conclude with the name of Jesus Christ, asked me very submissively who he was? I answered the son of God, of whom he had heard three days ago, that he had offered himself up a sacrifice to his father, for mankind; therefore we ought to praise God in his name, and in his name to ask for whatever it is lawful for us to desire: but of this, added I, I shall speak to you more fully hereafter.

CHAP. V.

She embarks with the Indians for their country; expounds the scriptures to them, and translates the Bible and Common Prayer into the Indian language. Visits her island.

WHILST these things past, I considered, that as I was entering upon an affair of the utmost importance, it would be highly necessary to commence with prayer. I was indeed sensible that it would be, in a great measure, very unintelligible to the Indians, yet I could not be satisfied with the omission, and thought I might pray in such a manner as that they, at least, would understand that I was desiring God to do them good. I therefore stood up, and told them, I would pray to God to be good to them, and that they were all to kneel down, as I did. But that they might not think I prayed to the statue, I got up to the top of the steps, and there kneeled down, with my back to the statue, and my face towards the people; and endeavoured to level my language, as well as I could, to their understandings; whilst the whole multitude showed great attention.

As I could sing very well, having learnt whilst I was in England, and had composed several hymns in the Indian language, as soon as I had done praying, I stood up and sung. It is not to be expressed how the whole multitude were affected, showing every decent expression of joy. I now told them I was ready to attend them to their own country. On this they set up a shout of gladness. I desired that some body would carry my bundle. I then set out in company with all the priests, followed by the multitude to the sea-side, where I saw a great number of canoes. I entered into one of them, and immediately the whole company entered into theirs. During our little voyage, I could not help reflecting upon the bold undertaking in which I had engaged; nor was I without my fears. But in my heart recommending myself to providence, I reassumed my courage, and fortified my mind.

When we approached the destined shore, it was covered with the natives, who, when I landed, respectively prostrated themselves to the earth. I, in return, bowed my body to them. I observed that they viewed my address with particular attention; whilst the priests conducted me to a little town full of small huts or cottages, into one of the best of which I was desired to enter. This, by the preparations that had been made, I supposed was designed for my residence. Here I found half a dozen Indian maids appointed to attend me, who, on my entrance, kneeled before me, till I ordered them to arise. These presented me with dried fish and flesh, fruits and flowers, and different liquors, as appeared from the look of them; for I took nothing but some fruit, of a kind, different from any I had seen upon my own island; for I was still on an island, though much larger. After I had been here some time, with the priests, I expressed my desire to be left alone, and that I should be glad to see the priests the next morning.

How greatly was my situation changed! From a solitary being, obliged to seek my own food from day to day, I was attended by a whole nation, all ready to serve me; and no care upon me but how to discharge the important business of an apostle, which I had now taken upon me. To this purpose, besides my daily instructing the priests in the knowledge of Christianity, I once a week taught the people in public; who I found very ready, and tolerably capable, to receive my instructions.[1]

As to the priests, I had expected much difficulty with them, and no little opposition; but was very agreeably surprized. They were very attentive, quick of apprehension, fond of instruction, and very ready to give me what assistance they could in teaching the people. The use I made of them was this; I mean the young priests, for the high priest was mostly confined at home, by the infirmities of his great age. The use, I say, I made of the young priests was to teach the children, and young people, the church of England's catechism: for as I had found a Common Prayer Book, among the few books that were in my chest, I translated the catechism into the Indian tongue, with a short and plain comment upon it; this I taught the priests to read, who afterwards made the children get it by

---

1 Compare to the change in Crusoe's role on the island following his encounter with Friday and others; Appendix A.2.iii.

heart. And as I had a Bible, I, at my leisure, translated that also, beginning with the plainest parts first, till I had finished the whole.[1]

I from time to time read the Bible in public to them, and, as I was able, explained it. I cannot but say I found myself very happy, among these plain, illiterate, honest people. There was nothing that they could do to please me, but they did it; and often expressed their hope, of my never leaving them. I found the manner of introducing myself among them was highly serviceable to me: for though, in every respect, they could not but observe that I was like them; yet it was easy to discover, that they conceived me more than a mere mortal. However, I did not think it my duty, any more than my interest, to undeceive them, as this opinion secured to me that respect and authority which were necessary for me to preserve, in order to carry on the great work among them, in which I was engaged.[2]

I sometimes amused myself in shooting with my bow and arrows, in which I exceeded any of them. But even this circumstance, trifling as it was, raised their opinion of me. In the summer season, I now and then went to visit my old island; but whenever I did so, I always ordered the Indians who rowed me over, to wait with the canoe by the sea-side; or to return home and fetch me in the evening, whilst I roamed about at my own pleasure.

When the same time returned next year, at which season they used to visit the oracle, the priests asked me, in the name of the people, if they should go to visit the oracle. I answered by no means, for that they would never more hear any answers from it.

I passed near two years very agreeably among them; in which I not only finished the translation of the Bible, as well as that of the Catechism, but indeed of most of the prayers in the Common Prayer-Book. I also had made a great progress in

---

1 John Eliot's complete translation of the Bible into Algonquian was printed in 1663. As a Puritan, however, he would not have sanctioned use of the Anglican Book of Common Prayer, much less translated it.

2 Alain-René Lesage's *Chevalier de Beuchêne* (1732) also incorporates an American Indian utopia and the character of a female missionary.

instructing the people; whom I happily brought off from their idolatry, to the knowledge of the true God, and to a tolerable idea of the christian religion. We now regularly observed the Lord's day, according to divine appointment. Though I had no right to administer the sacrament of the Lord's supper, yet I was well satisfied, that under the circumstances we were in, I might baptize. But I never did so, till I was well satisfied that the party had a tolerable notion of the christian religion, and earnestly desired to be baptized.

I could not help making one observation, and that a very just one. I remembered when I was in England, that I used to look into some of the deistical writers in my uncle's study. These writers laboured to prove, that Christianity was repugnant to plain uncorrupted reason. Yet I found this assertion intirely false; for, here a people, who had no other guide but their reason, no sooner heard Christianity plainly and firmly expounded to them, but they soon embraced it. And I am fully persuaded that whenever any unprejudiced person tries the religion of Christ by his reason, though he may find it in some measure above his reason, he yet will not find it contrary to it, and that it is worthy of his assenting to it.

But to continue my history. In the beginning of the third summer of my being here, not having been for a long time at my old island, on account of the late rainy season, answerable to winter in Europe, I ordered some Indians to row me thither, early in the morning. I told the Indians they might return back, and come again in the evening.

Every time I made this visit, I always went into my subterraneous apartments, to get some rings to distribute among the Indians. I suppose they wondered how I came by them, but never asked me. And, that they might have no suspicion that I brought them from the island, I never gave them any on my return to them; but always a few days before I intended a visit to my old habitation.

CHAP. VI.

*Lands on her island, ascends the idol, perceives two Europeans
approach the statue, one of whom she finds to be her cousin. Speaks to
them from the oracle, and after several interrogations discovers herself.*

As soon then as I was landed I walked to the iron door, which
I always left covered with earth, and fastened after me, as soon
as I had struck a light. I commonly ascended into the oracular
statue, and used to sit there sometimes to view the island. I did
so this time; but how greatly was I surprised, when looking forward I saw some men advancing towards me! I soon perceived
that they were Europeans, and, as well as I could conjecture, at
the distance they were from me, Englishmen.

I supposed that they belonged to some ship, that had either
cast anchor off the island, upon some occasion, or other, or
were shipwrecked; nay, thought I, they may be pirates. Whatever might be the cause of their landing, I had much to fear.

Indeed I was safe where I was; but how was I to get home?
and to stay long in such a place I could not. My next fear was
for the poor Indians, who would come in the evening, and not
finding me by the shore, as usual, would no doubt come upon
the island, in search of me, and be taken for slaves. Nor might
the evil stop thus; their country might be discovered, and probably invaded, and numbers of the people be carried away into
slavery, and other injuries committed. Thus did my busy imagination create, as in a moment, evils that happily never came
into existence: for these strangers soon came forwards, as I supposed, to view the statue, and being come near enough to be
heard, one of them said to another, "We have indeed found a
strange thing; what can this huge statue be designed for?"

"I know not," replied one who stood by him, "nor can I take
pleasure in any discovery in a place where, no doubt, my dear
cousin was starved to death or devoured by beasts."

These words, and the voice, alarmed me. "Sure," cried I
within myself, "he speaks of me, and it is my cousin Winkfield."

As he came nearer, I thought more certainly it was he. I listened attentively to their conversation, in hopes to hear some-

thing that might confirm my suspicion. They stood still, I suppose, to examine the statue, when as often as one of them spoke, I was the more confirmed, by hearing and seeing him, that it was my uncle's son. "But how," cried I, "should he come here? how know I was left on this island?"

These reflections destroyed my first suspicions, and my former fears began to revive; when he who I supposed was my cousin, said, "Let us stand here no longer; but as this seems undoubtedly to be an uninhabited island, let us continue our search, and perhaps we may yet find the bones of my dear Unca Winkfield; and by burying them pay the last, and only, respect we can to her unhappy memory; for if some beast destroyed her, he hardly ate her bones."

I heard these last words, including my name, too distinctly any longer to doubt, whether the speaker was my cousin, or not, and perceiving the company, was walking away cried out, "Winkfield, stay!"

At these words my cousin started violently, and turning round, as they all did, said to his companion, "Surely, Charles, I was called!" "No doubt," replied his companion Charles, "but it must be some of our companions who called you; for this island is uninhabited: we have been over it enough to see its bounds."

Mr. *Winkfield*. "No, Charles; it was too loud a voice to be human. Did not you hear it, gentlemen?" *speaking to his company.*[1]

Company. "Yes, indeed; and it was like thunder."

The joy of finding my cousin raised my spirits, and I was determined to indulge an adventure which promised much pleasure, and continued as follows.

Mr. *Winkfield*. "Sure it must be the spirit of my dear cousin! My father, who you know is far from being superstitious, has often said, he believes, that upon very important occasions, departed spirits are suffered to appear again: O that I could hear the voice again!"

Unca Winkfield. "Is your father alive?"

Mr. *Winkfield*. "Hark! it speaks again, like thunder! amazing!

. 1   At this point, the narrative begins to shift toward the mode of dramatic dialogue.

– shall I answer? Yes I will. I hope so, he was alive a few months ago."

One of the company. "This is strange, indeed! But it may be dangerous to stay; you know not with whom you may be conversing, it may be an evil spirit, and may hurt us. I have heard of such; let us go."

Another of the company. "I think the same; and never heard that any departed spirit, if it did return upon any particular occasion, spoke with as thundering voice as this. Besides, look at that statue, it brings to my mind the oracles that we read of in ancient history; and, to my apprehension, the voice seemed to come from thence; and, perhaps, it may be true, as we have read, that devils speak from such kind of statues."

Mr. Winkfield. "You speak with reason; but, I think, I could be almost content to speak to the devil to hear news of my cousin."

Charles. "Fie, talk not so; let us commit ourselves to God, and wait a little to hear if it will speak again, and listen if the sound comes really from the statue; but do not speak any more to it."

I could not help being much diverted at their fears; but unwilling yet to discover myself, I however determined to dissipate their terrors; and beginning a midnight hymn of my uncle's composing, which my cousin had set notes to, and taught me to sing, they started when I begun; but as soon as my cousin distinguished the tune, and understood the words, he was calm, and made a motion to the company to be silent, and when I had done, said,

"An evil spirit would not sing such holy words. My father composed them, and I taught my cousin to sing them."

One of the company. "This is not to be accounted for; yet we read that Satan can transform himself into an angel of light."

Mr. Winkfield. "Away! I have no fears; I will speak to it. – Does my cousin Unca live?"

Unca. "She lives, and is happy."

Mr. Winkfield. "Perhaps, in heaven."

Unca. "No; she lives upon earth."

Mr. Winkfield. "Shall I ever see her?"

Unca. "You may."

Mr. *Winkfield.* "But when and where?"

Unca. "Here; and that soon too."

Mr. *Winkfield.* "Let me see her then."

Unca. "You shall, if you will do one thing."

Mr. *Winkfield.* "I will do any thing that"—

Charles. "Stop, be not rash; ask what you are to do before you promise. I am myself not without my suspicions."

Mr. *Winkfield.* "I was going to say, I would do any thing not unworthy of a christian."

Charles. "I am satisfied."

Mr. *Winkfield.* "If I may see my cousin I will do any thing not unworthy of a christian."

Unca. "What I shall require is worthy of a christian."

Mr. *Winkfield.* "Propose it then."

Unca. "It is only to continue all of you where you are, and do you sing your favourite hymn, and before you have done you shall see Unca. It begins,

> "Whilst thus the sun illumes our sphere,
>   And bids the earth bring forth,
>   O spirit, deign in me to rear
>   Fruits of superior worth."

Mr. *Winkfield.* "I will do it— But who, or what, Charles, can this invisible being be, who seems thus intimately to know me?"

Charles. "I know not— but its request is innocent and pious; therefore begin."

As this hymn was a pretty long one, I knew it would give me sufficient time to carry my design into execution; which was to go out of my subterranean passage, drest in my priestly habits, and with my staff and crown; for in this manner I always came upon these insular visits. As they stood, it would be impossible for them to see me ascend from the earth. I pleased myself much with the surprize they would be in, to see me in a dress of which they could form no expectation, nor conceive the meaning of. I must mention one circumstance more, which contributed not a little to surprise them.

I had found among my clothes a small parcel of brass wire, which I had to mend my cages, in which I was carrying over some curious birds to England. After I came to live among the Indians, I made a strange kind of musical instrument. It was a long narrow box, made of thin wood, with holes cut in it, and several pieces of brass wire, placed in a particular manner. This I used to place in a tree, and when the wind blew properly upon it, it would send out certain soft pleasant notes.[1]

I had a mind to try what effect it would have in the statue. I found out a method to fix it, opposite to the mouth, withinside of the statue, and when the wind sat right to blow into it, the sounds were very delightful, and might be heard I believe almost over the whole island. After I had made this discovery I always brought it with me, and placed it in the statue, and, if the wind stood properly, I was greatly entertained with its melodious sounds, as I walked up and down.

As I found the wind sat full against the statue, I placed the instrument before it, and heard it play with a loudness that I could not have borne long. This no doubt could not but give my visitors a new alarm; yet, from the nature of it, was less terrifying than my speaking had been, with such a magnifying voice, as the mechanism of the statue occasioned: and indeed they were greatly alarmed, which gave birth to the following dialogue, just as my cousin began to sing, as I was afterwards informed.

Mr. *Winkfield.* "Ha! how sweet, but strange are these sounds!"

Company. "Astonishing beyond conception!"

One of the company. "This can be no human artifice; the loudness of it exceeds the power of art. I wish we were safe aboard our ships. I never was credulous; but henceforth I shall believe every fairy tale, if I escape this adventure; which I much fear."

Mr. *Winkfield.* "Let us be men, at least, and reflect that we are come in an honest cause. I own these appearances are very

---

1   "By this description, and the use to which she applied her invention, it seems to have been of the same kind with that we now call Æolus's harp." – *Author's* / *"Editor's"* note.

extraordinary: but they may portend good as well as evil. Must every supernatural event terminate in evil? Why may not the interruption of the usual course of things be as well for good as hurt?"

Charles. "True – Let us construe the omen in our favour, and be composed, and let Mr. Winkfield sing the hymn he promised."

Their conversation was so earnest, that they did not perceive me advancing, taking a slope till I got behind them, though at some distance, just as my cousin began his hymn. I stood still till he had done, in hopes they would see me before I walked up quite close to them; for I was afraid of alarming them too much. As soon as my cousin had finished his hymn, and all, looking at the statue, had stood silent some minutes, my cousin exclaimed,

"I have sung the hymn, but where is Unca?"

As he said these words, I moved gently towards the left, and then walked forwards, till I came upon a line with them. The musick still sounding, I then stopped, holding my staff so that the image of the sun, on the top of it, prevented a full view of my face. Presently, he who was called Charles saw me; when starting aside, he cried,

"Bless me! what is that?"

Upon this all turned and saw me, to their great surprize. They stood still and silent like mutes. I now bowed my staff as saluting them, and exposed my face to their full view, not very far from them, when my cousin, in his turn, exclaimed,

"It is my cousin's face! but can it be her?"

Unca. "It is."

Mr. *Winkfield.* "And living too?"

Unca. "Yes, cousin, and living too;" and smiling, added, "but have you forgot all your gallantry, and must I make the first advance?"

Having said this, I began, slowly, to step forward, when one of the company cried out,

"Nay, if you all have a mind to stay till the devil comes to you, I will not;" and ran away as fast as he could.

I still kept slowly moving on, whilst my cousin, and the rest, stood amazed, half leaning back, as if in doubt whether to stay or run after their companion. Their great amazement confounded me. I was at a loss what to say or do. I stopt short, and all of us stood silently gazing, them at me, and I at them. At last recovering from the confusion their great surprize had thrown me into, I addressed my cousin in these words:

Unca. "Dear cousin Winkfield, be not so much alarmed, I am really your cousin Unca Eliza Winkfield."

Mr. *Winkfield.* "You indeed appear to be such; but the strange things which I have seen and heard to-day, and your no less extraordinary appearance, scarce leave me sufficiently master of my senses to form a right judgment of what I see and hear."

By this time I was got close up to him, for he stood like a statue, and giving my hand said,

"Cousin Winkfield, be composed, and satisfied, that it is your cousin Unca who speaks to you."

He then took me in his arms, embraced and kissed me, and as soon as his transports, at finding me, a little subsided he said,

"But, pray my dear Unca, what mean the huge statue; the monstrous voice, loud like thunder, that talked to me and sung; this loud musick, which I still hear; the strange rich dress I see you in, and how have you subsisted in this strange uninhabited place? or say whether it is not the abode of invisible spirits, who have wrought the wonderful things I have heard, and whether they have not been your guardians? and whether – "[1]

Unca. "Stop, dear cousin; you have asked too many questions, and such as cannot be answered in a hurry: and I have, on my part, my questions to ask you, for your appearance here is very surprizing to me. How you should know of my being here is what I cannot conjecture. But of these things we will talk together at our leisure, when you are more composed."[2]

---

1   This representation of an enchanted island filled with strange sounds is reminiscent of Shakespeare's *Tempest*.
2   Crusoe's rescue from the island is described in Appendix A.2.iv.

CHAP. VII.

One of the company, terrified at Unca's appearance, runs to the ship,
and makes such a report to the crew, that they refuse to take them on
board.

BY this time the company, being pretty well satisfied that I was
a mortal, which at first they doubted of, came up to us, and
wished us joy on our unexpected happy meeting. We thanked
them, and I assured them, they need not be under any uneasiness; for that they were perfectly safe where they were: for
however extraordinary what they had heard and seen might
appear to them, the whole was the effect only of natural causes.
They were too mannerly to contradict what I said; but I could
easily perceive that they did not believe me. However, I left
them to their suspicions for that time.

My cousin now briefly informed me, that one of the gentlemen in company, whom he called captain Shore, the very day I
was left on this island, took my ship and the captain of it prisoner; and had sent him to England to be tried: that captain
Shore, coming to England, at my cousin's request, consented to
bring him over in search of me; as he thought, from the
account that the captain had given him, he could find the
island, as he happily had. He added, the ship now lies at anchor,
on the part of the island behind the statue, or whatever it is, and
if you please I will conduct you on board; for by this time they
will expect us to dinner, and I reckon are not a little uneasy
about what may have befallen us; for I suppose our companion
has made a dreadful report.

I answered that I was entirely at his disposal for a few hours.
"For a few hours!" returned he briskly, "why, must my dear
Unca and I ever part again? You talk strangely; and once more
make me almost doubt the reality of what I see and hear."

"Yes, we must part for a little," answered I, "but I will soon
satisfy you on that head. But let us pass on; I attend you."

As we walked along I told him, that I had come over on a
visit to the island that morning, and that at night I was obliged
to return back to the island on which I had lived above two

years; or otherwise my friends there would be under great uneasiness at my absence. Thus we went on talking, till we came to the shore, when my cousin was greatly surprised at not seeing the boat.

"I ordered the boat," said he, "to wait for me here; and though Mr. Lock in his fright might take it to go on board, he should have sent it back, and there has been time enough for its return."

Upon which captain Shore took a glass out of his pocket to look at the ship, which rode at anchor, some distance off. "Bless me," said he of a sudden, "what do I see! they are preparing to set sail. Sure the crew have not mutinied." He then called to them as loud as he could, and waved his handkerchief. He then said, "They made a signal that they see me." In a little time after he saw the boat coming. It soon appeared; but as it came near to the shore, the sailors it seems heard the musick from the statue, as the wind blew directly off from the island; this, together with my tawny complexion, and strange dress, so terrified them, that they stopped rowing, and would come no nearer; when one of the sailors said,

"Mr. Lock said right, this is certainly some inchanted island, and I would not row a stroke nearer if it was for the king."

Second Sailor. "Nor I; for I hear the devil's bagpipes playing as loud as thunder."

Third Sailor. "Aye; and don't you see that she-devil there wrapt in gold?"

Fourth Sailor. "I suppose she is the devil's wife, and this is their wedding-day, which makes her so fine and have so much musick."

Fifth Sailor. "I don't fear all the devils in hell, for I am a good catholic; I have crossed myself, and prayed to St. Patrick. But the devil shan't catch me ashore for all that."

Sixth Sailor. "I wish though I had her devilship's gold crown and gown, I would go no more to sea."

Fifth Sailor. "You fool, if you had them in your hand, they would all turn to dust."

We were obliged to hear this strange dialogue before captain Shore could put in a word. At last, with much ado, he made them hear him; but neither threats nor fair words could prevail upon them to come nearer the shore, whilst I stayed there. One of them said, that Mr. Lock came on board in a terrible fright, and said, he had seen a monster as tall as the moon, that it talked and sung louder than thunder, and that if he had not run away, a she-devil would have run away with him; and as one of our men was rowing him back, they said, they saw a hundred devils fly away with you all into the air, whilst they saw a great devil playing upon the bag-pipes, and he said, that for that matter he played much better than ever he heard a Scotchman in his life.

We therefore called a council, and had agreed to sail directly, if captain Shore had not called to us.[1]

As soon as the sailor had done talking, I told my cousin that I would leave them, that they might go on board their ship, and try to undeceive the crew, and that I would meet him the next morning at the steps. My cousin was much concerned at this unexpected sudden separation; but it appeared absolutely necessary, and there was no time for deliberation; for the men threatened every moment to row back to the ship.

---

1 This sentence belongs to the spoken account in the preceding paragraph, delivered by one of the sailors on board the ship. The "we" refers therefore to the ship's crew. Like the paragraph before it, there is no use of quotation marks either to indicate spoken discourse, or consistently to differentiate speakers from each other.

CHAP. VIII.

Mr. Winkfield left on shore; and after relating what passed between him and the ship's company, Unca and he retire in the evening to the other island.

THUS I left them, lamenting my own folly for not having discovered myself in a less alarming manner. As soon as I was got out of sight, the sailors set up a shout of joy, whilst I pensively walked on to my subterraneous apartments. I hastened up into the statue, to remove the occasion, which had had no little effect in the late unlucky incident. Here I sat musing on what might be the consequences of this affair. They may perhaps, cried I, murder my cousin, or force him to return back immediately, and not suffer him to go aboard again; or, if they do, may sail away, and take him with them. Better had it been never to have seen him again, than thus to prove the occasion of his death, or of new vexation to myself. I might have concluded my life with ease and pleasure among the Indians; but if I see him no more, I shall have laid a fresh cause for uneasiness as long as I live, and drag out the remainder of my life in misery; a burden to myself, and useless to all around me. What, continued I, is human life? As a wave destroys in a moment the wave that preceded it, so often does the arising moment the joys of the last; never more to return. Thus destroyed, perhaps, is all my past happiness! The sun, which in the morning saw me happy, now beholds me mourning; shedding tears which perhaps must flow, till death stops the current. Nor shall mine flow alone; an aged father, with his afflicted consort, may mourn a lost son, and curse the hour in which they first knew me, the unhappy means of bringing their gray hairs with sorrow to the grave.

I had taken no refreshment, since I came upon the island, in the morning; and my grief was too great to let me think of any, till at last, fatigued with weeping and fasting, I grew faint. I then thought I would leave the place, and take some refreshment; but not till I had sought comfort of him who only can give it. Now finding my mind more composed, and having determined to banish every anxious thought, till I saw what the returning day might produce (for I purposed to come again the next morning) I made haste to get above ground.

I did so, and was walking to the place where I had put some provisions, till I might want them, when I found part of the evils that my mind foreboded but too true; for who should I see walking solitarily along towards the statue, but my poor cousin! He did not see me till I called to him.

"Cousin Winkfield," said I, "what have my fears proved true? will they not receive you on board?"

Mr. *Winkfield*. "No; but be not alarmed, my dear Unca, captain Shore will soon be here again, and if, in the mean time, I can be with you I shall be happy."

Unca. "But will not your father and mother be alarmed at your delay?"

Mr. *Winkfield*. "They will not: for as I supposed it would be uncertain how long I might be searching for you, if I ever found you, I desired two years absence."

Unca. "I am so far satisfied. But relate what happened after I left you on the shore."

Mr. *Winkfield*. "As soon as you had left us, the sailors waited till you was got out of sight, and then set up a great shout, which possibly you heard."

Unca. "I did hear it, and from that moment was filled with fears, lest they should murder you, or leave you on shore, as they have done."

Mr. *Winkfield*. "Weep not for me, my dear Unca, for to live with you I should be contented if he never returns."

Unca. "I feel the tenderness of your expression. But my manner of living, length of time hath rendered agreeable to me; but it would be very disgusting to you. Rather may you soon return to your native country, be happy and leave me"–

Mr. *Winkfield*. "Stop, dear cousin! nor talk of leaving you; I never can, nor"–

Unca. "Hold, this is the language of a lover, ill suited to the present time and circumstances. The day wears away apace, and I must soon leave this island. Let us consider how you are to be disposed of. In the interim, will you partake of such mean fare as I have here? for, I suppose, you have had no refreshment since morning any more than myself."

We then walked to where I had stored my provisions, and there sat down to our repast. I now desired him to continue his relation.

Mr. Winkfield. "I said the sailors shouted when you were out of sight, and instead of rowing up to us, as we expected, boldly told the captain, that they had sworn before they set out, not to bring me on board; being determined never to sail in company with, a man, who, as Mr. Locke told them, had talked and sang songs with the devil: and had it not been for us, you know, captain, said one of them, he would have brought a she-devil on board with him, and as soon as she was on board, to be sure captain, she would have sunk the ship, and flown away with us all – No, no, good captain, we are bad enough, indeed; but we won't keep the devil company neither; nor any of his cronies.[1] He may go after her devilship if he pleases, if he can catch her; for I saw her fly into the air. Did you not, Jack?"[2]

Jack. "Yes, that I did. And she has left a terrible stink of brimstone behind. Don't you all smell it?"

All. "Smell it! aye to be sure; do you think we have no noses?"

Captain Shore was in a great passion. He told them "they were mutineers, and, he supposed, wanted to run away with the ship." To this they replied,

"No, no, captain, though we don't like the devil's company, we are honest fellows; we don't want to run away with the ship; that would be going to the devil another way, and I warrant he would trim us for using his lady so ill. You are our captain, and we will take you on board, if you please; but Mr. Winkfield is only a passenger, and we are not obliged to take him."

---

1 Baine surveys Defoe's beliefs on devils, and she-devils in particular (50-51).

2 Although this paragraph begins in Mr. Winkfield's own voice, by this point he is speaking in the voice of sailors. The dialogue that follows does not always distinguish clearly between John Winkfield's voice and the voices of others whose speech he is recounting for Unca Winkfield. It must therefore be read as a kind of dialogue within a dialogue.

Finding there was no good to be done with them, I whispered the captain that I would stay on shore all night, at all events; but desired he would come to me in the morning, and let me know if he had brought them to reason. However, as I had not spoken to the sailors, I was willing to try what I could do with them. "Gentlemen," said I, "you are really under a great mistake; that gentlewoman, whom you call a she-devil, is my cousin. She was three years ago left upon this island by a rogue of a captain, who ran away with her ship."

Sailor. "Well, Sir, if she is not a devil, I suppose she is a witch, and that is as bad; and that made the captain set her on shore. And pray was that tall monster who sung and played upon the bag-pipes your cousin too? You know, Sir, we heard him play ourselves, and the devil could not play louder."

Mr. *Winkfield.* "I was confounded at this question, not knowing myself how to account for what I had heard. They saw my confusion, and laughed: I therefore once more told the captain I would leave them, and hoped to see him in the morning. So we shook hands, and parted; he looking at me with great concern. I remembered you said, you should not leave this place till night. I was therefore walking up to the statue, in order to wait there some time, in hopes of seeing you thereabouts; if not, I intended walking up and down in quest of you; but as I was going thither, I had the pleasure of hearing you call me."

Unca. "I am very glad you found me so soon, for the sun is declining apace; and if you had missed me you would have passed an uneasy night. For though there is here nothing to hurt you, you could not know that. But as we have done eating, let us go down to the sea-side, where a canoe will soon be ready to carry us where you shall pass the night in safety. In the morning we will return here, and I hope we shall see the captain, and hear that matters are made up on board. And as I suppose you are impatient to know what has happened to me since I was put upon this island, and to know the meaning of the extraordinary things that you have seen and heard, I will inform you as we go along."

CHAP. IX.

*They return in the morning to see whether the captain had brought
the crew to obedience; but find they had forced him to sail back to
Europe.*

WE now walked down to the sea-side, where two Indians waited with my canoe. They seemed surprised at the appearance of
a stranger, especially of a white man, as having never seen one
before. I quickly spoke chearfully, and told them, that he was a
relation of mine, who was come to see me. They seemed very
well satisfied, and asked no questions, as they were used to pay
an implicit regard to every thing I said. During our short voyage I made a brief relation of every thing that had befallen me
from my first being put upon the island to the time of my
cousin's arrival. He listened with an attention little short of
astonishment.

"What a series," cried he, "of amazing providences! I will
learn their language, and end my days in carrying on the great
work you have so wonderfully begun amongst them; for never
shall I be able so successfully to fulfil the duties of my function
as among a plain, uncorrupted, honest people as these I find
are; for since I saw you, Unca, I have entered into holy orders."

Unca. "The novelty of what you have heard, has heated your
imagination, and hurried you into a resolution, that in your
calmer moments you will retract. Besides, what will your parents say to their only son's becoming a voluntary exile?"

Mr. *Winkfield.* "They are too good to oppose so pious a
resolve. What a glorious harvest do I see! I will return, and ask
their leave. I know I shall obtain it. And then I shall have but
one thing more to ask, and that is, Unca's hand for ever, in
return for my heart, which she has long had – What says my
dear cousin?"[1]

Unca. "That we must land," returned I, very gravely, "for we
are upon the shore, and the Indians waiting for us."

I saw he was chagrined at this unexpected answer so foreign

---

1   Robinson Crusoe's eventual marriage is referred to in Appendix A.2.iv.

to his question; when, rising up, I gave him my hand to conduct me on shore, which he squeezed, as if he meant to punish
it for the mortification my tongue had given him. It was a fine
moon-light night, and there were a great many Indians waiting
for my return. Seeing a stranger with me, they looked as if in
doubt or fear, whether they should come up to me as usual.
Perceiving their condition, I called to them with that air of
affability with which I always spoke to them, telling them I had
brought a relation with me, who had come a great way to see
me.

Their usual joy at my presence now revived, and they came
up to us, shewing my cousin the same respect commonly paid
to me. They attended us to my hut. I desired two of the priests
to sup with us, that no offence might be given by being alone
with a man: though such was the chaste simplicity of their
manners, and their high opinion of me, that I believe the precaution was unnecessary; for suspicion reigns most in guilty
hearts, and chiefly with regard to those we think meanly of.
My cousin was pleased with his repast, though but the second
time he had ever partaken of such kinds of provisions. The
priests, who had learned a little English of me, were mightily
pleased whenever they understood a word that my cousin said,
and most highly so as often as they could make themselves
understood. When it was time to go to rest, the priests took
care to provide a proper place for my cousin.

We were up the next day very early, breakfasted, and then set
out for the island. During our voyage, the night before, I was
the chief speaker; but now, in his turn, my cousin briefly told
me how he came to know where I was; of which hereafter.

Nor did he omit any opportunity in the course of his narration to give me to understand, that he had all along preserved
that affection for me that he had formerly professed. But as
often as he dropped such expressions, I took care to show no
particular regard to them, but only a general attention to the
thread of his discourse.

When we had reached the island I ordered the Indians not
to return as usual, not knowing what sudden occasion I might
have for them; but strictly charged them not to advance a foot

forward into the island, nor to row to any other part of it. My cousin and I now crossed the island to the place where we expected the boat to come to. We sat and walked up and down here, by turns, till noon, but saw no boat. We then took some of the provisions we had brought, and dined. In short, we passed the whole afternoon, till it was time to think of returning home, without seeing any signs of a boat: we therefore feared the crew had mutinied, and run away with the ship, and may be murdered the captain and the other passengers; at least, that they would not suffer the captain to come on shore again. The evening being far advanced, we were obliged to return home, not a little chagrined at our disappointment.

My concern, indeed, arose upon my cousin's account, for had the ship arrived I would not have gone away in it, being determined to live and die amongst my dear Indians.[1] Nor, indeed, was it his intention to have gone home in her, but to have sent word to his parents that he had found me, and was determined to live and die with me; which, however, as often as he mentioned it, I most strongly opposed.

My cousin insisted upon his going without me the next morning, to which I was forced to agree; but was greatly surprised to see him return before noon. "What means this quick return?" cried I; "I cannot conjecture the occasion."

Mr. *Winkfield*. "It seems," said he, "as if providence, though by a somewhat adverse stroke, designs that I shall carry my resolution to teach the Indians into practice, and spend my days with my dear Unca, whether she will or no; for as I drew near, this morning, to the part of the shore where we yesterday waited for the boat, I saw, as I thought, several chests, and casks, and such, indeed, they were: and when I came up to them, I beheld a stick fixed in the ground, to the top of which was tied a letter. This I took, and found it directed to me. Here it is.

"Sir,
"I solemnly assure you, that I have done every thing in my power, both by threats and promises, to induce the crew to let

---

1 Compare to the fate of Crusoe's island and its inhabitants; see Appendix A.2.iv.

me fetch you on board; but in vain: so deeply has Mr. Locke's foolish reports wrought upon their superstitious minds; for which indeed he is now very sorry. All that I can obtain is, that they will carry all your goods, and put them on shore by break of day, to-morrow, provided they see nothing of your cousin, as I hope they will not, and that you may at least have your goods, which no doubt you will want. As the men were only hired to come here, they insist upon returning to Europe. Please God I arrive safe there, I will give your father and mother the best account I can. As your cousin has found means of subsisting, I hope you will too. I intend to come again in search of you next year; for it will be impossible to come sooner. I remember your cousin said her residence was on another island, where I suppose you will live also.

"If I am so happy as to live to come again, I will set up an high pole, in some conspicuous part of the island with a streamer; so that if you come from time to time to look for me, you will be sure to know when I am arrived; but you must not expect me much short of a year hence. But as I know not at what part of the island I may be obliged to cast anchor, or at what distance from it, when I arrive, I will place a small piece of cannon on the shore nearest to where the ship may lie, that if you come whilst we are on board, you may by firing it, give notice of your being upon the island. I most heartily wish your cousin and you health and happiness, and hope we shall meet again; nor to that end shall any thing be wanting that may be in the power of,

Sir, &c. &c."

I was heartily sorry at reading of this; but my cousin smiled, and said he should now live with me whether I would, or not. "I am," added he, "only uneasy for my father and mother; but I know when they are assured that you are living, and that we are together, their concern will be greatly lessened, and they will comfort themselves with the pleasing hope of hearing of us both next year. And it is in your power, my dear Unca, greatly to add to their pleasure, by enabling me to acquaint them, that you have become their daughter. Let us then be united in the glorious work you have begun; teach me the Indian language, and I will join the glorious task you have commenced, and tread, with you, the path that leads to glory and happiness by well doing. One motive for my seeking you was, that, if we should meet, we might be for ever united. Consider one thing more, that if you refuse me, we cannot enjoy those hours of privacy together, I at least shall wish for, without offence to those around us; at least I know your delicacy will be hurt by them."

This last remark had some weight with me, yet I declined a direct answer; for though I loved him as a friend and relation, I had never considered him as a lover; nor any other person. It appeared to me, indeed, as if it must be as he would have it, yet the reflection gave me no pleasure; for though the Indians, I believed, would not entertain any ill suspicions of my conduct, yet I could not satisfy myself with the reflection of being much alone with a man, as it hurt my modesty. However, postponing the matter for further consideration, my immediate care was to provide a sufficient number of canoes, the largest that could be got, to fetch my cousin's baggage.

CHAP. X.

Embark their effects for the inhabited island. Mr. Winkfield marries
his cousin, and proceeds in the work of conversion. He relates by what
means he came to the knowledge of her being in that part
of the world.

THE next morning my cousin set out with a sufficient number
of canoes, and brought all his things over. Besides a proper
stock of clothes for himself, and some useful books, he had, as if
certain of finding me living, and the naked inhabitant of a desolate island, brought over apparel for me. The linen indeed was
very acceptable to me, as I now began to be in great want of it.

I was very much pleased to see a basket with about a dozen
live fowls, cocks and hens; with these the island was soon
stocked, and were very pleasing to the Indians, who had never
seen any before. But what were these to the many other things
the Indians had never seen before, at which they wondered, and
were delighted with? a gun and the surprising effects of gun-
powder, a telescope, and many other European curiosities, and
without which indeed they were sufficiently happy![1] However,
the sight of these raised in them an high opinion of my cousin,
next to that they had for me.

I passed my time happily enough, before my cousin's arrival,
but more so afterwards; for from his presence I enjoyed a new
advantage. We now had divine service every Lord's day; which
my cousin performed in English, and I was interpreter, till he
had learned the Indian language, which he did much sooner
than could have been well expected; and at last preached in the
Indian tongue. I had now the great pleasure of once more
enjoying all the ordinances of the church, and the constant
company of a religious and sensible companion, to whom,
through his constant importunity, I was at last obliged to give

---

1   See Appendix B.1.i. This novel ascribes a kind of nostalgic dimension to the Indi-
    ans' existence prior to their encounter with European technology that is not
    present in the original sources, and that reflects the emergence of primitivism,
    romanticism, and the figure of the noble savage.

my hand, about two months after his arrival.[1] We first married ourselves according to the church rites, the high-priest acting as father, who died about a week after. We were also married according to the custom of the Indians, that they might the more perfectly be satisfied, their form having nothing in it contrary to our religion.

From the time of my cousin's settling here, or rather my husband, as I must now for the future call him, the Indians were properly baptized, married, and many of them, at their earnest desire, admitted to the Lord's supper. My husband and I spent much of our time in teaching the christian religion to the children; he the boys and I the girls; so that, what with catechising, and his preaching twice a week, we had greatly the appearance of a christian country. The natural simplicity and purity of the Indian manners greatly accelerated this work.

Being now more at leisure, I desired my husband to recount to me at large, what he had at first but briefly told me of, concerning his learning where I was, and of the captain who had robbed me, and set me on the uninhabited island. It was thus:

"There came one day," said my husband, "a sea-faring man to my father, who enquired of him if he had not a niece at Virginia of the same name with himself. To this my father replied, that he had a brother, and niece, at that place, if they were not come away, for that he had expected them some months, his brother having sent over great part of his effects, which he had received, and who had informed him by letter, that he and his daughter would soon follow; but, added he, do you, Sir, know any thing of them?"[2]

"Yes, Sir," replied the stranger: "your brother, I am sorry to inform you, died just as he was about to set out for England."

---

1   The anti-romantic character of the Winkfields' marriage bears contrasting to contemporaneous English novels such as Richardson's *Pamela*.

2   Again, Winkfield Jr.'s account of previous events is presented as a series of dialogues within a dialogue that makes it difficult to distinguish speakers from each other. In the following account, John Winkfield Jr. tells a story heard by his father, the minister Winkfield Sr., who tells a story told by an unnamed stranger who is the captain of a merchant ship, who tells a story told by a pirate, who is revealed to be Captain Shore.

Mr. *Winkfield senior.* "I am very much concerned to hear of my dear brother's death – But as to my niece, does she intend to come over to England, or to continue there? perhaps she has sent you with orders concerning her effects."

Stranger. "As to your niece, I do not come from her. I never was at Virginia in my life, nor did I ever see her: yet I have some news to acquaint you with concerning her; but which I am sorry to say will give you much concern."

Mr. *Winkfield senior.* "Indeed, after hearing of the death of my brother, I shall be still farther grieved to hear of any affliction that may have befallen my dear niece but God's will be done: pray let me hear it, whatever it is."

Stranger. "I shall be ready to give you all the information that I can about her. But as I cannot do so in a few words, I must beg your patience, whilst I relate to you circumstantially all the particulars that I know.

"I am, Sir, a captain of a merchant-ship. As we were sailing from the West-Indies for this my native country, we met with a sail, which fired a gun for us to bring to. This alarmed us; for as it was a time of peace, I feared it might be a pirate, as indeed it proved; but happily one from whom we received not the least injury, as you will hear.

"We were, in no wise, capable of defending ourselves, the pirate being a ship of force: we, therefore, were obliged to suffer them to come a-board us. As soon as the captain got upon deck, he addressed himself to me in these words:"

Pirate. "Be not alarmed: I am, indeed, a pirate, but design no hurt to you. I come on board only to ask a favour, which you can easily grant, if you, as I see you are my countryman, are bound to England; if not, I will return to my own ship, and leave you unmolested to pursue your own course."

Merchant Captain. "I am bound, Sir, for England, and if I can render you any service there, will readily and faithfully do it."

Pirate. "If you please, I will go into your cabin with you, and there open my business more fully."

Merchant Captain. "According to his request, captain Shore, (for that he told me was his name) and his mate, and I, retired into my cabin, when he soon resumed his discourse in this manner."

Captain *Shore*. "I was a few years ago, as I find you are, a merchant captain; but having very bad success, I proposed to my mate, here, to turn pirate, to which he consenting, we broke our intentions to the crew, who too readily agreed to our proposal. However, we all resolved never to commit a murder, and rather quit our prey than kill any, if we could not otherwise get master of them: and this resolution we have happily kept to this moment. We have been very successful in our robberies. But not daring to put into any port in these parts, and as little to return to England, we sought for, and found, a small uninhabited island, where we stored our treasures, and at times resided. This was very privately situated, and where we were in no danger of being discovered, and lay very convenient to put to sea from, and retreat to, as we saw occasion.

"The last prize we made was in this manner. Discovering a small ship, we, as usual, made what sail we could till we came pretty near to her, and then fired a gun for her to bring to. As she was a ship of no force, and we had our guns out ready to fire upon her, she immediately surrendered. As soon as we came on board, we saw an Indian hanging up alive, and bleeding at the yard-arm. I asked the captain the meaning of this cruel treatment. He replied, that he was a very wicked fellow, and had thrown him over-board, and that he and five others of his countrymen had conspired to murder all the crew, and run away with the ship; but that he and his men had overpowered and killed the five others. Though this seemed very plausible, such things often happening at sea, yet I could not help observing a confusion in the countenance of the captain, which destroyed the credit of his story. Naturally abhorring cruelty, and suspecting something bad, I ordered the Indian to be immediately taken down, and his wounds to be dressed. Being determined to make what enquiry I could into this affair, I ordered the captain, and the poor Indian to be carried, for indeed he could not walk, to go down into the cabin with me and my mate: and here a dismal scene presented! the floor and wainscot of the cabin all smeared with blood, and two female Indians wounded and bleeding, who seemed to start with horror at the sight of the captain. Having imposed silence on the captain, I ordered the women to give me an account of what had happened, which, as well as, their fright and weakness would permit, they did; and the poor Indian, in a few words, not being able to speak much, confirmed what the women had said: but the captain absolutely denied their relation, and appealed to the crew, who confirmed his denial.

"But suspecting the captain to be guilty"–

Here Mr. Winkfield senior interrupted him somewhat peevishly. "Pardon me, Sir," cried he, "you are very prolix. I am confounded, and want to know what all this has to do with my niece; the part of the world, the slaves alarm me; let me know the worst at once: was my niece murdered, Sir, on board this ship?"

Merchant Captain. "No, Sir, she was not, and may be yet living for ought I know to the contrary."

Mr. *Winkfield senior.* "*May be yet living!* you talk mysteriously. I thought you came to tell me news about her, and you only say *she may be yet living* – I abhor suspense; if you know anything concerning her, tell it me at once."

Mr. *Winkfield junior.* "Honoured Sir, don't be in such a hurry, you will offend the gentleman, and we may never come to the perfect knowledge of this affair."[1]

Merchant Captain. "Sir I take no offence, I attribute your father's interruption to his concern for his niece, but cannot give him the information he wants, except in the manner I was going to do it. If it be agreeable, I will proceed."

Mr. *Winkfield senior.* "I am of a warm temper, Sir, the subject is very interesting, and in affection I know no difference between my niece and my daughter; I hope therefore you will excuse my rude interruption, and be pleased to proceed in your own way."

Merchant Captain. "I am satisfied. I left off I think, with saying that notwithstanding the captain's denial of what the Indi-

---

1 Here Winkfield Jr. is recounting his own words delivered in the earlier context of the conversation between his father and the merchant captain.

ans accused him of, and though backed by his crew, that captain Shore still thought him guilty."

Mr. *Winkfield senior.* "You did, good Sir, what am I next to hear? poor Unca!"

Merchant Captain. "I was determined, said captain Shore, to come to the bottom of this affair, and therefore made every inquiry that I could. The account the Indians gave me was this, that their mistress's name was Unca Eliza Winkfield; that her father, a very rich man, had lately died at Virginia; that she was coming over to England to an uncle, her father's brother, a clergyman; that she had great riches on board the ship; and that the ship also was her's, which she had promised to give upon her arrival in England to the captain, who took care of it for her, and who was a poor broken man; that the captain would have forced her to sign a bond, to marry his son upon their arrival in England, where he lived; that upon her absolute refusal to sign this bond, he threatened to put her upon some uninhabited island. Saying this in the hearing of her male-slaves, who loved her dearly, he who had been hanged up at the yard-arm, and another, threw the captain out of the cabin window into the sea; but that swimming to the ship, he was taken up again, when at the head of his men he came into the cabin, murdered five of the male Indians, and hung the sixth up at the yard-arm, intending there to let him die; and then put their mistress upon a desolate island, and was proceeding to sail away with the ship and all their mistress's effects."

CHAP. XI.

Continues his relation. Some account of captain Shore, who resolves to leave off his piratical practices.

"HAVING heard this relation," continued captain Shore, "I immediately searched among the goods on board, and found sufficient proofs that they belonged to Mrs. Winkfield.

"However, I was determined, if possible, to make the captain confess his guilt: looking therefore very sternly, I gave orders that my men should take and hang him up at the yard-arm, where the poor Indian had lately hung, and there to remain till he should confess his crime, or die; when he, seeing my command was going to be carried into execution, immediately acknowledged his crime, and, falling down at my feet, besought my pardon. No, cried I, if the innocent could find no mercy, the guilty shall not. You was[1] deaf to the cries of the injured Mrs. Winkfield, and I will be deaf to yours; you shall be hanged.

"At the instant I uttered this command these words of Scripture came strong upon my mind, suddenly like lightning, *Thou are inexcusable, O man, whosoever thou art, that judgest: for wherein thou judgest another, thou condemnest thyself: for thou that judgest doest the same things. And thinkest thou this, that thou shalt escape the judgment of God?*[2] I was so sensibly struck with these words, that I started up, as in a fright, from my seat. What, cried I to myself, am I doing? is such a wicked wretch as I am a proper person to set in judgment upon another? I have not murdered indeed, but how many robberies have I not committed? My heart was changed, as it were in a moment, I saw my own wickedness, abhorred myself, and repented. But concealing my confusion, as well as I could, from those about me, I turned about to the captain, and said, I will not take upon myself to execute the sentence upon you that your crimes deserve; but I will take care to have you and your men sent to England, there to be tried by the laws of your own country.

---

1 Were.
2 Romans 2:1-3.

"I then ordered that he should be secured, and all his men, and to make the best of our way with both ships to our island. When we arrived there, I ordered all possible care to be taken of the three Indians. But the poor Indian who had been hung up, died in a few days. Whilst he lived, he greatly lamented the fate of his mistress, and almost his last words were, *Pray hang the wicked captain*. As to the females they soon recovered, their wounds being but slight.

"The day after we reached our island, I told my mate what had passed in my mind the day before; and that I was determined to leave off the evil course I had unhappily engaged in, at all events. He seemed much affected with what I said, and, after pausing some time, answered, But how shall we be able to extricate ourselves? Where go to live with safety?

"To this I replied, that I was determined to save my soul, if I could not my body, and would sooner get, by some means or other, to England and be hanged, than continue the life I had led. For I considered the words that came into my mind yesterday as no less than the words of God. To this my mate replied, I am not a little affected with what happened to you yesterday, and do pray that I may be enabled to follow you in so good a resolution; and may God give to us both, *a repentance not to be repented of*. But what shall we do with our men?[1]

"I answered, I have not been without my thoughts concerning them. You know they all love me much, and are not such wicked men as most of their profession commonly are. And I have at times heard them lament their long absence from their families, and now and then express some dislike at the unhappy way they are in. I intend therefore to talk to them, and to propose a way by which possibly we may all obtain our pardon, and return again to our own country.

"Accordingly the same evening I called them all together, and, my mate being present, thus addressed them:

"My dear countrymen!

"I once was so unhappy, and so wicked, as to persuade you to join with me in the evil course, which we have but too suc-

---

1   Cf. Appendix A.2.iv, in which Crusoe leaves several criminals behind on his island.

cessfully followed for some years. What distress, by our robberies, have we brought upon many innocent persons? But
how much greater distress will come upon us, unless we most
seriously repent of our sins? You know what happened, yesterday, on board the ship, we took. Whilst I was, in presence of
some of you, reproving that wicked man, my own conscience
smote me with these words of holy writ, *Thou are inexcusable, O
man, whosoever thou art, that judgest: for wherein thou judgest another, thou condemnest thyself: for thou that judgest doest the same things.
And thinkest thou this, that thou shalt escape the judgment of God?*

"From that moment it was, I hope, given me to repent, and I
am determined to break off my sins, let the event be what it
will. As I once led you into the ways of sin, happy should I be,
if I might recover you to the paths of virtue. Consider, though
we have hitherto escaped the vengeance of man, we cannot
escape that of God. Nor, indeed, can we in all probability, to
the end, escape the justice of man. The wretch who yesterday
no doubt gloried in his success over an innocent, helpless
woman, before night fell into our hands, and has lost his liberty,
and the riches for which he damned his soul. Let his fate be a
warning to us before the like befalls us: I have thought of a
method by which we may very probably escape the punishment due to our crimes, do a noble piece of justice, and have an
opportunity, if God shall please to bless it, to repent.

"It is to keep the prisoners we took yesterday close confined
on board their own ship, and to secure that and the treasure in
it, and to draw up the whole account of this affair to send it to
the injured lady's uncle in England, acquainting him that if he
will apply to king James, and procure a pardon for us, that we
may return to England, upon condition that we bring the captain and all his crew there, that they may suffer for their crimes,
and deliver up to the lady's uncle the ship and all effects on
board. This no doubt will be complied with. To carry this
scheme into execution, is to stop the first small ship that we
may meet with going to England; I will tell the captain our situation, and desire him to take me on board, and set me down
on the coast of Holland or France, as maybe most convenient,
where I may wait in safety, whilst he carries my letters to England, and till I can receive the conditional pardon and a passport

for myself and you to return to England in a convenient limited time; which, as soon as I receive, I will hire a small sailing-vessel, and make what haste I can to you, that we may once more see our native country. As we have always divided among ourselves what we have taken, if I reach England, I will publish my return, with an offer to restore the effects I have unjustly taken, to such persons as can satisfy me that I robbed them, though I should have nothing left. For if I don't do so, I shall doubt the sincerity of my own repentance; for there can be no true repentance without restitution. As to you, I must leave it to your own consciences, whether you will follow my example, or not. But God grant you may! Consider what I have said, and may God direct you, and tomorrow give me your answer.[1]

"They accordingly came to me the next morning, when they all expressed their hearty consent to my proposal. Though I could not but observe, that this unanimity of opinion proceeded from different motives; in some it arose only from fear of being caught and hanged, in others, from a desire of enjoying their ill gotten wealth: but I had the pleasure to find that a few were touched with what I had said, and seemed to manifest signs of repentance.

"I answered, that since they were come to this resolution, our immediate business was to watch for the opportunity, and that when it offered, I told them, that they must be sure to continue upon the island till I should return, unless I staid so long as to give them good reason to conclude, that some accident had happened to me. This they all most solemnly promised to do.

"And now, Sir, said captain Shore, speaking still to me,[2] the wished-for opportunity offers, if you please to afford it; but I lay you under no restraint; for though I wish you may grant my desire, you are at your liberty. If you have any reason to object to it, you are welcome to pursue your voyage in peace and safe-

---

1 Captain Shore's speech to his crew concludes here; with the following paragraph we return to his conversation with the merchant captain, who of course is telling this story to the Winkfields in England.
2 The "me" here is the merchant captain.

ty; for I will not offer the least injury to you, or any with you."

"For my part, answered I, I am very ready to give you all the assistance in my power, towards carrying so good a resolution into action, and as I have some business to transact upon the coast of France, I can very conveniently land you there, and when I arrive in England will diligently and faithfully execute what commission you shall please to give me."

"Well then," replied captain Shore, "I will go on board my own ship, and get together such things as I want, and return to you, that we may proceed upon our voyage. In the mean time, Sir, in order to remove any bad impressions that your crew may have conceived of me, be pleased to inform them that I did not stop you as a pirate, but only to request the favour of a passage to France. I promised I would do so;[1] and accordingly did; and they were all well satisfied.

"As soon as captain Shore returned on board with his baggage, we set sail, and when we arrived upon the coast of France, I there left him, and, being myself[2] returned safe to England, have waited on you. And here, Sir, continued the strange captain to my[3] father, is a letter from captain Shore to you, bills of parcels of the goods on board your niece's ship, and some other papers belonging to your niece."

---

1 The "I" of this sentence is the merchant captain; the "I" of the previous sentences in this paragraph is Captain Shore.
2 This "myself" is the merchant captain.
3 This "my" is Winkfield Jr., although the sentence he is recounting here is in the voice of the merchant captain.

CHAP. XII.

After captain Shore had obtained a pardon for himself and crew, he returns in search of Mrs. Winkfield. Fate of the captain who left her on the uninhabited island. They resolve to settle their affairs in England, and live with the Indians. Conclusion.

"MY father and I heard this wonderful relation with great attention and surprise; but still mourned for you, my dear Unca, being ignorant of your fate. However, we proceeded to bring the captain to justice. The case was laid before the king and council, together with captain Shore's petition, on behalf of himself and people. I got the conditional pardon granted, having three years allowed to bring home the ship and crew, with a proper passport.

"As soon as captain Shore received notice of this, he came home to England, in order to hire a ship to carry him back to his people.

"Whilst he was making the proper preparations for his voyage, we were much together. I asked him, as he was well acquainted with those parts where my cousin had been left upon some island or other thereabouts, whether he thought it improbable to discover the island.

"He answered, I know those parts extremely well, and I doubt not, that if the captain[1] will give me the best account of the situation of the island that he can, but that I should be able to find it out.[2] This gave me great pleasure. Well then, said I, if my father and mother will give their consent, I will go along with you in quest of her.

"It is not impossible, added I; but she may be yet living. I have read of as surprising deliverances; at the worst we may find her bones, and pay the last honours to her dear unhappy memory: and here, my dear Unca, I wept indeed!

---

1 I.e., the captain who abandoned Unca Eliza Winkfield and whom Shore hung from the yard-arm.
2 The "I" of this sentence is Shore; the "me" and "I" of the following two sentences are spoken by Winkfield Jr.

"My father and mother consented with pleasure, and as soon as every thing was settled, and ready, we sailed. We had a speedy and prosperous voyage to the captain's island; where he and the pardon he brought were highly welcome. I there saw the wicked captain, who robbed you. He gave captain Shore a very clear account of the situation of your island. We staid here no longer than till your ship and the captain's were ready to sail for England with your treasure, and the prisoners all under his mate's command. We promised to follow them soon, to our native country. We then set sail for your island, and happily discovered it; but, what was a much happier discovery, found you alive and well."

Thus my husband ended his extraordinary relation;[1] full of a wonderful series of providences. At length the time arrived to expect the return of captain Shore; and now my husband went twice every week over to the island for three months; but no appearance of any ship. But at last as he approached the shore one morning, he saw a streamer playing in the air; he knew the signal, and rejoiced. But walking to the place where he first landed out of the ship that brought him, he saw no cannon, nor any body upon the island; he continued walking along the shore, yet saw no ship. At last he spied a cannon; having always a tinder-box ready about him for the expected occasion, he struck a light, and fired the cannon. It was not long before he saw a boat making for the shore, and soon discovered that captain Shore was one of the company. They were very glad to see each other. It seems captain Shore had arrived but the day before, when he set up the flag, and having waited all day, left the cannon ready charged before he returned on board. My husband went on board the captain's ship, and dined with him, when they agreed that captain Shore should come with my husband to our island, and spend three days with us. We[2] were both very glad to hear that our father and mother were all well, and our sisters.

---

1 Here the text returns to the first-person narrative of its heroine.
2 The narration here shifts to the plural first person; it does not revert again to the singular first person of Unca Winkfield until the final paragraph of the text.

We desired captain Shore to relate the particulars that had happened from the time he left the island, which he did, as follows:

Captain Shore. "I shall pass over the unimportant accidents that occurred during our voyage. Upon our arrival in England, I found all your family well. They were amazingly surprised to hear of Mrs. Winkfield's being alive. And the thought of your being together made them easy as to their not seeing their son again with me, as they expected. But when I told them of the strange things that I had seen and heard on the island, they were confounded. I know not, said your father, what to make of these things; they exceed human comprehension. Surely your fears and surprise made you to imagine things to exist that really did not. May be so, returned I, willing to drop a subject, that I myself did not understand, and which if insisted on, might have given great uneasiness.

"I should have returned much sooner here, continued captain Shore; but as my ship, and Mrs. Winkfield's were both arrived a week before me, I was obliged to stay till the cargoes were landed, and what belonged to Mrs. Winkfield committed to your father's care.[1] Besides, I was obliged to attend the trial of the captain and the crew, who were found guilty upon their own confession.[2] The captain, and three of his men, were hanged at Execution-Dock, and afterwards hung in chains; the rest of the crew were transported for life.[3] As soon as this was over, I, and my men, took out our pardons in due form. They afterwards went where they pleased. Several persons, who I had robbed at sea brought in their claims, all which I fully

---

1 Thus William Winkfield's New World fortunes, inherited from Unca's Indian mother, are transported to the Old World and into patriarchal hands. See Appendix A.2.iv for Robinson Crusoe's economic fate.

2 That is, the captain and crew who abandoned Unca Winkfield and killed or wounded her slaves.

3 Execution Dock, located in East Wapping, was one of several sites in and outside of London where hangings took place. The bodies of those convicted of particularly aggravated crimes were sometimes hung in chains for public display after they were executed. Criminals who escaped hanging were often transported, that is, banished to foreign lands and sentenced to indentured labour.

answered. These things settled, I set out in Mrs. Winkfield's ship, and arrived safe at your first island."

In return to captain Shore's relation, we acquainted him with every thing that we had done in his absence, and satisfied his curiosity about the wonderful things that he had met with upon the island. When we had finished our account, the captain expressed great surprise and satisfaction at what had happened, and added, "Since what has befallen me, I shall not like to reside in England, nor any more to be concerned in worldly affairs; therefore if you think me a true convert, let me join in your society. We replied, that we had no doubt of his sincerity, and should be very glad of his company."

We now agreed captain Shore and my husband should return together to England, that my husband might take a final leave of his relations, receive his parents blessing, and settle half of his and my fortune upon his sisters, and leave the rest for charitable uses, and bring over such books and things as might be useful to us in our retirement. But we first determined to go upon my island, to collect all the gold treasure there, to blow up the subterraneous passage, and the statue, that the Indians might never be tempted to their former idolatry. When all this was done, and the golden treasure put on board, the captain and my husband set out upon their voyage.[1] They arrived safe in England, saw our father and mother, who consented to their son's request, and gave him their blessing. As soon as my husband had sold his golden treasure, and settled his affairs, and bought a large library of books, and many kinds of goods and linen, he and captain Shore once more returned to me. We ordered the sailors to unload their cargo upon my first island, and to leave us a large boat for the more convenient conveying our goods to the other island, where we lived. We did not suffer the sailors to come any farther upon the island, than just to land the goods, that no discovery of our habitation might be made. As we never intended to have any more to do with Europe, cap-

---

1 This destruction and plunder is reminiscent of Cortés's conquest of Mexico. McDowell suggests that the representation of Indians in *The Female American* combines North American with South American sources (309).

tain Shore and my husband ordered a person who came for that purpose, to return to Europe with the ship, by whom, for my father and mother's satisfaction, I sent over these adventures.

FINIS.[1]

---

1   The 1767 London edition contains a final list of other titles sold by the printers of this novel.

Appendix A: "English" Sources

The early English novel created for audiences in both England and America some of the most popular representations of the New World and its inhabitants. Behn's *Oroonoko; or, The Royal Slave* (1688), for example, is the earliest English novel written about and set in the Americas. Narrated by a woman who claims to have been "an Eye-witness" to the tragic tale of the slave hero Oroonoko, the novel represents one of the earliest literary depictions in narrative of Native Americans, emphasizing their prelapsarian innocence and the corrupting effects of their contact with Europeans. Defoe subsequently set his enormously popular tale of Robinson Crusoe's shipwreck on a deserted island near the river "Oroonoque" in South America. Many of the concerns with religion, race, and colonialism embedded in *Robinson Crusoe* (1719) were elaborated more pointedly by Defoe in *Serious Reflections During the Life ... of Robinson Crusoe* (1720). The second of two sequels Defoe wrote to his earlier novel, *Serious Reflections* records meditations by an older Crusoe on his earlier voyages, including his reflections on religion in the New World. Among the best-known of Defoe's early imitators was Peter Longueville, who in *The Hermit* (1727) tells the story of Philip Quarll, shipwrecked on a deserted island where he lives for fifty years. Like its predecessor *Crusoe* and the later *The Female American*, Longueville's novel engages concerns with literary authenticity, the economics of isolation, and piety.

1. Aphra Behn

i. *Oroonoko*, selections, 3-4

This Adornment, with their[1] long black Hair, and the Face painted in little Specks or Flowers here and there, makes 'em a wonderful Figure to behold. Some of the Beauties, which

---

1 The female narrator is describing the natives of Surinam in the West Indies.

indeed are finely shap'd, as almost all are, and who have pretty Features, are charming and novel; for they have all that is called Beauty, except the Colour, which is a reddish Yellow; or after a new Oiling, which they often use to themselves, they are of the Colour of a new Brick, but smooth, soft and sleek. They are extreme modest and bashful, very shy, and nice of being touch'd. And though they are all thus naked, if one lives for ever among 'em, there is not to be seen an undecent Action, or Glance: and being continually us'd to see one another so unadorn'd, so like our first Parents before the Fall, it seems as if they had no Wishes, there being nothing to heighten Curiosity; but all you can see, you see at once, and every moment see; and where there is no Novelty, there can be no Curiosity....

And these People represented to me an absolute *Idea* of the first State of Innocence, before *Man* knew how to sin: And 'tis most evident and plain, that simple Nature is the most harmless, inoffensive and vertuous Mistress. 'Tis she alone, if she were permitted, that better instructs the World, than all the Inventions of Man: Religion wou'd here but destroy that Tranquillity they possess by Ignorance; and Laws wou'd but teach 'em to know Offence, of which now they have no Notion. They once made mourning and fasting for the Death of the *English* Governor, who had given his Hand to come on such a day to 'em, and neither came nor sent; believing, when a Man's word was past, nothing but Death cou'd or shou'd prevent his keeping it: And when they saw he was not dead, they ask'd him what Name they had for a Man who promis'd a thing he did not do? The Governor told them, Such a Man was a *Lyar*, which was a Word of Infamy to a Gentleman. Then one of 'em reply'd, *Governor, you are a Lyar, and guilty of that Infamy*. They have a native Justice, which knows no Fraud; and they understand no Vice, or Cunning, but when they are taught by the *White* Men.

ii. *Oroonoko*, selections, 4–5

With these People, as I said, we live in perfect Tranquillity, and good Understanding, as it behoves us to do; they knowing all the places where to seek the best Food of the Country, and the means of getting it; and for very small and unvaluable Trifles, supply us with that 'tis impossible for us to get.... And then for shooting, what they cannot take, or reach with their Hands, they do with Arrows; and have so admirable an Aim, that they will split almost an Hair, and at any distance that an Arrow can reach: they will shoot down Oranges, and other Fruit, and only touch the Stalk with the Dart's Point, that they may not hurt the Fruit. So that they being on all occasions very useful to us, we find it absolutely necessary to caress 'em as Friends, and not to treat 'em as Slaves, nor dare we do other, their numbers so far surpassing ours in that Continent.

2. Daniel Defoe

i. *Robinson Crusoe*, selections, 3-8

Being the third Son of the Family, and not bred to any Trade, my Head began to be fill'd very early with rambling Thoughts: My Father, who was very ancient, had given me a competent Share of Learning, as far as House-Education, and a Country Free-School generally goes, and design'd me for the Law; but I would be satisfied with nothing but going to Sea, and my Inclination to this led me so strongly against the Will, nay the Commands of my Father, and against all the Entreaties and Perswasions of my Mother and other Friends, that there seem'd to be something fatal in that Propension of Nature tending directly to the Life of Misery which was to befal me.

My Father, a wise and grave Man, gave me serious and excellent Counsel against what he foresaw was my Design. He call'd me one Morning into his Chamber, where he was confined by the Gout, and expostulated very warmly with me upon this Subject: He ask'd me what Reasons more than a meer wandring Inclination I had for leaving my Father's House and my native Country, where I might be well introduced, and had a Prospect of raising my Fortunes by Application and Industry, with a Life of Ease and Pleasure. He told me it was for Men of desperate Fortunes on one Hand, or of aspiring, superior Fortunes on the other, who went abroad upon Adventures, to rise by Enterprize, and make themselves famous in Undertakings of a Nature out of the common Road; that these things were all either too far above me, or too far below me; that mine was the middle State, or what might be called the upper Station of *Low Life*, which he had found by long Experience was the best State in the World, the most suited to human Happiness, not exposed to the Miseries and Hardships, the Labour and Sufferings of the mechanick Part of Mankind, and not embarass'd with the Pride, Luxury, Ambition and Envy of the upper Part of Mankind....

I was sincerely affected with this Discourse, as indeed who could be otherwise? and I resolv'd not to think of going abroad any more, but to settle at home according to my Father's Desire. But alas! a few Days wore it all off; and in short, to prevent any of my Father's farther Importunities, in a few Weeks after, I resolv'd to run quite away from him....

It was not till almost a Year after this that I broke loose, tho' in the mean time I continued obstinately deaf to all Proposals of settling to Business, and frequently expostulating with my Father and Mother, about their being so positively determin'd against what they knew my Inclinations prompted me to. But being one Day at *Hull*, where I went casually, and without any Purpose of making an Elopement that time; but I say, being there, and one of my Companions being going by Sea to *London*, in his Father's Ship, and prompting me to go with them, with the common Allurement of Seafaring Men, *viz.* That it should cost me nothing for my Passage, I consulted neither Father or Mother any more, nor so much as sent them Word of it; but leaving them to hear of it as they might, without asking God's Blessing, or my Father's, without any Consideration of Circumstances or Consequences, and in an ill Hour, God knows. On the first of *September* 1651 I went on Board a Ship bound for *London*; never any young Adventurer's Misfortunes, I believe, began sooner, or continued longer than mine. The Ship was no sooner gotten out of the *Humber*, but the Wind began to blow, and the Winds to rise in a most frightful manner; and as I had never been at Sea before, I was most inexpress-

ably sick in Body, and terrify'd in my Mind: I began now seriously to reflect upon what I had done, and how justly I was
overtaken by the Judgment of Heaven for my wicked leaving
my Father's House, and abandoning my Duty; all the good
Counsel of my Parents, my Father's Tears and my Mother's
Entreaties came now fresh into my Mind, and my Conscience,
which was not yet come to the Pitch of Hardness to which it
has been since, reproach'd me with the Contempt of Advice,
and the Breach of my Duty to God and my Father.

ii. *Robinson Crusoe*, selections, 45–53

The last Time of these two had well near been fatal to me; for
the Sea having hurried me along as before, landed me, or rather
dash'd me against a Piece of a Rock, and that with such Force,
as it left me senseless, and indeed helpless, as to my own Deliverance; for the Blow taking my Side and Breast, beat the Breath
as it were quite out of my Body; and had it returned again
immediately, I must have been strangled in the Water; but I
recover'd a little before the return of the Waves, and seeing I
should be cover'd again with the Water, I resolv'd to hold fast
by a Piece of the Rock, and so to hold my Breath, if possible,
till the Wave went back; now as the Waves were not so high as
at first, being nearer Land, I held my Hold till the Wave abated,
and then fetch'd another Run, which brought me so near the
Shore, that the next Wave, tho' it went over me, yet did not so
swallow me up as to carry me away, and the next run I took, I
got to the main Land, where, to my great Comfort, I clamber'd
up the Clifts of the Shore, and sat me down upon the Grass,
free from Danger, and quite out of the reach of the Water....
    I walk'd about on the Shore, lifting up my Hands, and my
whole Being, as I may say, wrapt up in the Contemplation of
my Deliverance, making a Thousand Gestures and Motions
which I cannot describe, reflecting upon all my Comerades
that were drown'd, and that there should not be one Soul sav'd
but my self; for, as for them, I never saw them afterwards, or any
Sign of them, except three of their Hats, one Cap, and two
Shoes that were not Fellows....

After I had solac'd my Mind with the comfortable Part of my Condition, I began to look round me to see what kind of Place I was in, and what was next to be done, and I soon found my Comforts abate, and that in a word I had a dreadful Deliverance: For I was wet, had no Clothes to shift me, nor any thing either to eat or drink to comfort me, neither did I see any Prospect before me, but that of perishing with Hunger, or being devour'd by wild Beasts; and that which was particularly afflicting to me, was, that I had no Weapon either to hunt and kill any Creature for my Sustenance, or to defend my self against any other Creature that might desire to kill me for theirs: In a Word, I had nothing about me but a Knife, a Tobacco-pipe, and a little Tobacco in a box, this was all my Provision, and this threw me into terrible Agonies of Mind, that for a while I run about like a Mad-man; Night coming upon me, I began with a heavy Heart to consider what would be my Lot if there were any ravenous Beasts in that Country, seeing at Night they always come abroad for their Prey.

All the Remedy that offer'd to my Thoughts at that Time, was, to get up into a thick bushy Tree like a Firr, but thorny, which grew near me, and where I resolv'd to set all Night, and consider the next Day what Death I should dye, for as yet I saw no Prospect of Life; I walk'd about a Furlong from the Shore, to see if I could find any fresh Water to drink, which I did, to my great Joy; and having drank and put a little Tobacco in my Mouth to prevent Hunger, I went to the Tree, and getting up into it, endeavour'd to place my self so, as that if I should sleep I might not fall; and having cut me a short Stick, like a Truncheon, for my Defence, I took up my Lodging, and having been excessively fatigu'd, I fell fast asleep, and slept as comfortably as, I believe, few could have done in my Condition, and found my self the most refresh'd with it, that I think I ever was on such an Occasion....

When I came down from my Appartment in the Tree, I look'd about me again, and the first thing I found was the Boat, which lay as the Wind and the Sea had toss'd her up upon the Land, about two Miles on my right Hand....

... and having consider'd well what I most wanted, I first

got[1] three of the Seamens Chests, which I had broken open and empty'd, and lower'd them down upon my Raft; the first of these I fill'd with Provision, *viz.* Bread, Rice, three Dutch Cheeses, five Pieces of dry'd Goat's Flesh, which we liv'd much upon, and a little Remainder of *European* Corn which had been laid by for some Fowls which we brought to Sea with us, but the Fowls were kill'd; there had been some Barly and Wheat together, but, to my great Disappointment, I found afterwards that the Rats had eaten or spoil'd it all; as for Liquors, I found several Cases of Bottles belonging to our Skipper, in which were some Cordial Waters, and in all about five or six Gallons of Rack, these I stow'd by themselves, there being no need to put them into the Chest, nor no room for them. While I was doing this, I found the Tyde began to flow, tho' very calm, and I had the Mortification to see my Coat, Shirt, and Wast-coat which I had left on Shore upon the Sand, swim away; as for my Breeches which were only Linnen and open knee'd, I swam on board in them and my Stockings: However this put me upon rummaging for Clothes, of which I found enough, but took no more than I wanted for present use, for I had other things which my Eye was more upon, as first Tools to work with on Shore, and it was after long searching that I found out the Carpenter's Chest, which was indeed a very useful Prize to me, and much more valuable than a Ship Loading of Gold would have been at that time; I got it down to my Raft, even whole as it was, without losing time to look into it, for I knew in general what it contain'd.

My next Care was for some Ammunition and Arms; there were two very good Fowling-pieces in the great Cabbin, and two Pistols, these I secur'd first, with some Powder-horns, and a small Bag of Shot, and two old rusty Swords; I knew there were three Barrels of Powder in the Ship, but knew not where our Gunner had stow'd them, but with much search I found them, two of them dry and good, the third had taken Water, those two I got to my Raft, with the Arms, and now I thought my self pretty well freighted, and began to think how I should get

---

1 From the boat which he has boarded by means of a raft.

to Shore with them, having neither Sail, Oar, or Rudder, and the least Cap full of Wind would have overset all my Navigation....

My next Work was to view the Country, and seek a proper Place for my Habitation, and where to stow my Goods to secure them from whatever might happen; where I was I yet knew not, whether on the Continent or on an Island, whether inhabited or not inhabited, whether in Danger of wild Beasts or not: There was a Hill not above a Mile from me, which rose up very steep and high, and which seem'd to over-top some other Hills which lay as in a Ridge from it northward; I took out one of the fowling Pieces, and one of the Pistols, and an Horn of Powder, and thus arm'd I travell'd for Discovery up to the Top of that Hill, where after I had with great Labour and Difficulty got to the Top, I saw my Fate to my great Affliction, (*viz.*) that I was in an Island environ'd every Way with the Sea, no Land to be seen, except some Rocks which lay a great Way off, and two small Islands than this, which lay about three Leagues to the West.

I found also that the Island I was in was barren, and, as I saw good Reason to believe, un-inhabited, except by wild Beasts, of whom however I saw none, yet I saw Abundance of Fowls, but knew not their Kinds, neither when I kill'd them could I tell what was fit for Food, and what not; at my coming back, I shot at a great Bird which I saw sitting upon a Tree on the Side of a great Wood, I believe it was the first Gun that had been fir'd there since the Creation of the World; I had no sooner fir'd, but from all the Parts of the Wood there arose an innumerable Number of Fowls of many Sorts, making a confus'd Screaming, and crying every one according to his usual Note; but not one of them of any Kind that I knew: As for the Creature I kill'd, I took it to be a Kind of a Hawk, its Colour and Beak resembling it, but had no Talons or Claws more than common, its Flesh was Carrion, and fit for nothing.

iii. *Robinson Crusoe*, selections, 202-06; 212; 216-17; 241

I observ'd, that the two[1] who swam, were yet more than twice as long swimming over the Creek, as the Fellow was, that fled from them: It came now very warmly upon my Thoughts, and indeed irresistibly, that now was my Time to get me a Servant, and perhaps a Companion, or Assistant; and that I was call'd plainly by Providence to save this poor Creature's Life; ... I slowly advanc'd towards the two that follow'd; then rushing at once upon the foremost, I knock'd him down with the Stock of my Piece; I was loath to fire, because I would not have the rest hear; though at that distance, it would not have been easily heard, and being out of Sight of the Smoke too, they wou'd not have easily known what to make of it: Having knock'd this Fellow down, the other who pursu'd with him stopp'd, as if he had been frighted; and I advanc'd a-pace towards him; but as I came nearer, I perceiv'd presently, he had a Bow and Arrow, and was fitting to shoot at me; so I was then necessitated to shoot at him first, which I did, and kill'd him at the first Shoot; the poor Savage who fled, but had stopp'd; though he saw both his Ene-mies fallen, and kill'd, as he thought; yet was so frighted with the Fire, and Noise of my Piece, that he stood Stock still, and neither came forward or went backward .... at length he came close to me, and then he kneel'd down again, kiss'd the Ground, and laid his Head upon the Ground, and taking me by the Foot, set my Foot upon his Head; this it seems was in token of swearing to be my Slave for ever....

But that which astonish'd him most, was to know how I had kill'd the other Indian so far off, so pointing to him, he made Signs to me to let him go to him, so I bad him go, as well as I could, when he came to him, he stood like one amaz'd, looking at him, turn'd him first on one side, then on t'other, look'd at the Wound the Bullet had made, which it seems was just in his Breast, where it had made a Hole, and no great Quantity of Blood had follow'd, but he had bled inwardly, for he was quite dead; He took up his Bow, and Arrows, and came back....

---

1   "Savages" who are pursuing another "savage" who has escaped from them.

He was a comely handsome Fellow, perfectly well made; with straight strong Limbs, not too large; tall and well shap'd, and as I reckon, about twenty six Years of Age. He had a very good Countenance, not a fierce and surly Aspect; but seem'd to have something very manly in his Face, and yet he had all the Sweetness and Softness of an *European* in his Countenance too, especially when he smil'd. His Hair was long and black, not curl'd like Wool; his Forehead very high, and large, and a great Vivacity and sparkling Sharpness in his Eyes. The Colour of his Skin was not quite black, but very tawny; and yet not of an ugly yellow nauseous tawny, as the *Brasilians*, and *Virginians*, and other Natives of *America* are; but of a bright kind of dun olive Colour, that had in it something very agreeable; tho' not very easy to describe. His Face was round, and plump; his Nose small, not flat like the Negroes, a very good Mouth, thin Lips, and his fine Teeth well set, and white as ivory. After he had slumber'd, rather than slept, about half an Hour, he wak'd again, and comes out of the Cave to me; for I had been milking my Goats, which I had in the Enclosure just by: When he espy'd me, he came running to me, laying himself down again upon the Ground, with all possible Signs of an humble thankful Disposition, making a many antick Gestures to show it: At last he lays his Head flat upon the Ground, close to my Foot, and sets my other Foot upon his Head, as he had done before; and after this, made all the Signs to me of Subjection, Servitude, and Submission imaginable, to let me know, how he would serve me as long as he liv'd; I understood him in many Things, and let him know, I was very well pleas'd with him; in a little Time I began to speak to him, and teach him to speak to me; and first, I made him know his Name should be *Friday*, which was the Day I sav'd his Life; I call'd him so for the Memory of the Time; I likewise taught him to say *Master*, and then let him know, that was to be my Name....

... I believe, if I would have let him, he would have worshipp'd me and my Gun: As for the Gun it self, he would not so much as touch it for several Days after; but would speak to it, and talk to it, as if it had answer'd him, when he was by himself;

which, as I afterwards learn'd of him, was to desire it not to kill him....

During the long Time that *Friday* has now been with me, and that he began to speak to me, and understand me, I was not wanting to lay a Foundation of religious Knowledge in his Mind; particularly I ask'd him one Time who made him? The poor Creature did not understand me at all, but thought I had ask'd who was his Father; but I took it by another handle, and ask'd him who made the Sea, the Ground we walk'd on, and the Hills, and Woods; he told me it was one old *Benamuckee*, that liv'd beyond all: He could describe nothing of this great Person, but that he was very old; much older he said than the Sea, or the Land; than the Moon, or the Stars: I ask'd him then, if this old Person had made all Things, why did not all Things worship him; he look'd very grave, and with a perfect Look of Innocence, said, *All Things do say O to him*: I ask'd him if the People who die in his Country went away any where; he said, yes, they all went to *Benamuckee*; then I ask'd him whether these they eat up went thither too, he said yes.

From these Things, I began to instruct him in the Knowledge of the true God: I told him that the great maker of all Things liv'd up there, pointing up towards Heaven: That he governs the World by the same Power and Providence by which he had made it: That he was omnipotent, could do every Thing for us, give every Thing to us, take every Thing from us; and thus by Degrees I open'd his Eyes. He listned with great Attention, and receiv'd with Pleasure the Notion of *Jesus Christ* being sent to redeem us, and of the Manner of making our Prayers to God, and his being able to hear us, even into Heaven; he told me one Day, that if our God could hear us up beyond the Sun, he must needs be a greater God than their *Benamuckee*, who liv'd but a little way off, and yet could not hear, till they went up to the great Mountains where he dwelt, to speak to him; I ask'd him if ever he went thither, to speak to him; he said no, they never went that were young Men; none went thither but the old Men, who he call'd their *Oowacakee*, that is, as I made him explain it to me, their Religious, or

Clergy, and that they went to say *O*, (so he called saying Prayers) and then came back, and told them what *Benamuckee* said: By this I observ'd, That there is *Priestcraft*, even amongst the most blinded ignorant Pagans in the World; and the Policy of making a secret Religion, in order to preserve the Veneration of the People to the Clergy, is not only to be found in the *Roman*, but perhaps among all Religions in the World, even among the most brutish and barbarous Savages.

I endeavour'd to clear up this Fraud, to my Man *Friday*, and told him, that the Pretence of their old Men going up the Mountains, to say *O* to their God *Benamuckee*, was a Cheat, and their bringing Word from thence what he said, was much more so; that if they met with any Answer, or spake with any one there, it must be with an evil Spirit: And then I entred into a long Discourse with him about the Devil, the Original of him, his Rebellion against God, his Enmity to Man, the Reason of it, his setting himself up in the dark Parts of the World to be Worship'd instead of God, and as God; and the many Strategems he made use of to delude Mankind to his Ruine; how he had a secret access to our Passions, and to our Affections, to adapt his Snares so to our Inclinations, as to cause us even to be our own Tempters, and to run upon our Destruction by our own Choice....

My Island was now peopled, and I thought my self very rich in Subjects; and it was a merry Reflection which I frequently made, How like a King I look'd. First of all, the whole Country was my own meer Property; so that I had an undoubted Right of Dominion. *2ndly*, My People were perfectly subjected: I was absolute Lord and Law-giver; they all owed their Lives to me, and were ready to lay down their Lives, *if there had been Occasion of it*, for me. It was remarkable too, we had but three Subjects, and they were of three different Religions. My Man *Friday* was a Protestant, his Father was a *Pagan* and a *Cannibal*, and the *Spaniard* was a Papist: However, I allow'd Liberty of Conscience throughout my Dominions: But this is by the Way.

iv. *Robinson Crusoe*, selections, 273-78

I was at first ready to sink down with the Surprize. For I saw my Deliverance indeed visibly put into my Hands, all things easy, and a large Ship just ready to carry me away whither I pleased to go. At first, for some time, I was not able to answer him[1] one Word; but as he had taken me in his Arms, I held fast by him, or I should have fallen to the Ground....

Then I took my Turn, and embrac'd him as my Deliverer; and we rejoyc'd together. I told him, I look upon him as a Man sent from Heaven to deliver me, and that the whole Transaction seemed to be a Chain of Wonders; that such things as these were the Testimonies we had of a secret Hand of Providence governing the World, and an Evidence, that the Eyes of an infinite Power could search into the remotest Corner of the World, and send Help to the Miserable whenever he pleased....

After these Ceremonies past, and after all his good things were brought into my little Apartment, we began to consult what was to be done with the Prisoners we had; for it was worth considering, whether we might venture to take them away with us or no, especially two of them, who we knew to be incorrigible and refractory to the last Degree; and the Captain said, he knew they were such Rogues, that there was no obliging them, and if he did carry them away, it must be in Irons, as Malefactors to be delivered over to Justice at the first *English* Colony he could come at; and I found that the Captain himself was very anxious about it.

Upon this, I told him, that if he desir'd it, I durst undertake to bring the two Men he spoke of, to make it their own Request that he should leave them upon the Island: *I should be very glad of that*, says the Captain, *with all my Heart....*

When the Captain was gone, I sent for the Men up to me to my Apartment, and entred seriously into Discourse with them of their Circumstances, I told them, I thought they had made a right Choice; that if the Captain carry'd them away, they would certainly be hang'd. I shewed them the new Captain, hanging

---

1   The captain of a ship that has arrived on shore.

at the Yard-Arm of the Ship, and told them they had nothing less to expect.

When they had all declar'd their Willingness to stay, I then told them, I would let them into the Story of my living there, and put them into the Way of making it easy to them: Accordingly I gave them the whole History of the Place, and of my coming to it; shew'd them my Fortifications, the Way I made my Bread, planted my Corn, cured my Grapes; and in a word, all that was necessary to make them easy: I told them the Story also of the sixteen *Spaniards* that were to be expected; for whom I left a Letter, and made them promise to treat them in common with themselves.

I left them my Fire Arms, *viz.* Five Muskets, three Fowling Pieces, and three Swords. I had above a Barrel and half of Powder left; for after the first Year or two, I used but little, and wasted none. I gave them a Description of the Way I manag'd the Goats, and Directions to milk and fatten them, and to make both Butter and Cheese....

And thus I left the Island, the Nineteenth of *December*, as I found by the Ship's Account, in the Year 1686, after I had been upon it eight and twenty Years, two Months, and 19 Days; being deliver'd from this second Captivity, the same Day of the Month, that I first made my Escape in the *Barco-Longo*, from among the *Moors* of *Sallee*.

In this Vessel, after the long Voyage, I arriv'd in *England*, the Eleventh of *June*, in the Year 1687, having been thirty and five Years absent.

v. *Robinson Crusoe*, selections, 285; 304–06

I was now Master, all on a Sudden, of above 5000 *l. Sterling* in Money, and had an Estate, as I might well call it, in the *Brasils*, of above a thousand Pounds a Year, as sure as an Estate of Lands in *England*: And in a Word, I was in a Condition which I scarce knew how to understand, or how to compose my self, for the Enjoyment of it....

I was now to consider which Way to steer my Course next, and what to do with the Estate that Providence had thus put into my Hands, and indeed I had more Care upon my Head now, than I had in my silent State of Life in the Island, where I wanted nothing but what I had, and had nothing but what I wanted: Whereas I had now a great Charge upon me, and my Business was how to secure it....

In the mean time, I in Part settled my self here; for first of all I marry'd, and that not either to my Disadvantage or Dissatisfaction, and had three Children, two Sons and one Daughter: But my Wife dying, and my Nephew coming Home with good Success from a Voyage to *Spain*, my Inclination to go Abroad, and his Importunity prevailed and engag'd me to go in his Ship, as a private Trader to the *East Indies*: This was in the Year 1694.

In this Voyage I visited my new Collony in the Island, saw my Successors the *Spaniards*, had the whole Story of their Lives, and of the Villains I left there . . .

Besides this, I shar'd the Island into parts with 'em, reserv'd to my self the Property of the whole, but gave them such Parts respectively as they agreed on; and having settled all things with them, and engaged them not to leave the Place, I left them there.

From thence I touch'd at the *Brasils*, from whence I sent a Bark, which I bought there, with more People to the Island, and in it, besides other Supplies, I sent seven Women, being such as I found proper for Service, or for Wives to such as would take them: As to the *English* Men, I promis'd them to send them some Women from *England*, with a good Cargoe of Necessaries, if they would apply themselves to Planting, which I afterwards perform'd. And the Fellows prov'd very honest and diligent after they were master'd, and had their Properties set apart for them. I sent them also from the *Brasils* five Cows, three of them being big with Calf, some Sheep, and some Hogs, which, when I came again, were considerably encreas'd.

vi. *Serious Reflections*, selections, 221–22; 227

If we take the north part of America, exclusive of all the country which the Spaniards possess, and which they call the empire of Mexico, and exclusive too of what the English and French possess on the coast and in the two rivers of Canada and Mississippi as above, which indeed are but trifles, the rest of that country, which, as far as it has been travelled into, is found exceeding populous, is a great deal larger than all Europe ... – I say this vast continent, full of people, and no doubt inhabited by many millions of souls, is all wrapt up in idolatry and paganism, given up to ignorance and blindness, worshipping the sun, the moon, the fire, the hills their fathers, and, in a word, the devil.

As to the thing we call religion, or the knowledge of the true God, much less the doctrine of the Messiah and the name of Christ, they not only have not, but never had the least intimation of it on earth, or revelation of it from heaven, till the Spaniards came among them; nay, and now Christians are come among them, it is hard to say whether the paganism is much abated except by the infinite ravages the Spaniards made where they came, who rooted out idolatry by destroying the idolaters, not by converting them....

Let but an open door be made for the preaching of the word of God, and the ministers of Christ be admitted, if they do not spread Christian knowledge over the face of the earth the fault will be theirs. Let but the military power reduce the pagan world, and banish the devil and Mahomet from the face of the earth, the knowledge of God be diligently spread, the word of God duly preached, and the people meekly and faithfully instructed in the Christian religion, the world would soon receive the truth, and the knowledge of Divine things would be the study and delight of mankind.

3. Peter Longueville *The Hermit* 182–84

About forty Paces further, he finds a Chest in a Clift of the Rock, which had been wash'd up there by the Violence of the late Storm: Heavens, said he, more fatal Effects of Fate's Cruelty and Man's Temerity! Was the Sea made for Men to travel on? Is there not Land enough for his rambling Mind to rove? Must he hunt after Dangers and put Death to Defiance? What is the

Owner of this the better for it now? Or, who can be the better in a Place so remote, and the Access to it so difficult, being not to be approach'd, but on the Wings of Providence, and over the Back of Death? Now, was this full of massy Gold, or yet richer Things, I thank my God, I am above the Use of it; yet I'll take it Home, it was sent here by Providence; perhaps for the Relief of some so necessitated and destitute; so goes to lift it, but could not, therefore was oblig'd to fetch his Hatchet to beat it open, that he might take away what was in it by degrees; so having taken as much of the Sail-Cloath as he could conveniently carry, with the few Oysters he had got, he went Home and fetch'd the Tool, wherewith he wrench'd the Chest open, from which he took a Suit of Cloaths and some wearing Linen, these, said he, neither the Owner, nor I, do want, so laid them down, the next Thing he took out, was a Roll of several Sheets of Parchment, being blank Indentures and Leases; these, said he, are Instruments of the Law, and often apply'd to Injustice; but I'll alter their mischievious Properties, and make them Records of Heavens Mercies, and Providence's wonderful Liberality to me; so instead of being the Ruin of some, they may chance to be the reclaiming of others: At the Bottom of the Chest lay a Rundlet of Brandy, a *Cheshire* Cheese, a Leather Bottle full of Ink, with a Parcel of Pens, and a Pen-Knife; as for these, said he, they are of Use, the Pens, Ink, and Parchment have acquip'd me to keep a Journal, which will divert and pass away a few anctious Hours; as for the Cheese and Brandy, they will but cause me new Cares, before I had 'em, I wanted 'em not; now, the Benefit and Comfort I shall find in them (when gone) will make me hanker after them most; I wish I had still been without 'em, but now they are here, it would be a Sin to let them be lost, I'll take them Home, and only use them at my need, which will both make them hold out the longer, and me grow less fond of them.

So by Degrees takes Home the Chest, and what was in it; and now having Materials to begin his Journal, he immediately fell to Work, that, for want of other Books, he might, at his Leisure, peruse his past Transactions, and the many Mercies he had receiv'd from Heaven; and, that after his Decease, whoever is directed there by Providence, upon reading his wonderful Escapes in the greatest of Dangers, his miraculous Living, when remote from human Assistance, that in the like Extremity they might not despair: Thus begins, from his being eight Years old (as well as he can remember he heard an old Aunt of his say) to the Day of his being Cast-away, which happen'd on the 10th of *July* 1675, being then twenty eight Years of Age, resolving to continue it to his Death.

Appendix B: "American" Sources

Although the three writers represented here were Englishmen, and their texts all published in England, their work is regularly labeled American and included in American literary anthologies. They are perhaps better distinguished from the sources in Appendix A, however, less by national identity than by genre. Thomas Hariot, George Percy, and John Smith all offered readers travel accounts and reports of the New World and its indigenous population, accounts that were proto-ethnographic rather than fictional. At the same time, these texts were no less limited by their writers' historical and cultural vision than subsequent novels were. Hariot's *Briefe and True Report*, for example, offered a detailed description of the potential commodities of the Roanoke colony in the Carolinas and of southern Algonquian religious practice. Hariot's account was first published in 1588, but was reprinted in 1590 with engravings by Theodore de Bry (which in turn were based on drawings and watercolors by John White). Sixteen years later, George Percy was among the group of Virginia settlers first led by Edward Maria Wingfield. Although Wingfield wrote his own account of the disputes and difficulties that afflicted the group and that eventually led to his overthrow, Wingfield's "Discourse" did not appear in print until 1845, while Percy's "Discourse" was included in Samuel Purchas's widely circulated travelogue *Hakluytus Posthumous; or Purchas His Pilgrimes* (1625). After Wingfield's demise, John Smith rose to prominence and power in Jamestown, and gained further recognition in England as the author of a number of travel narratives. Among the most famous of these was his *Generall History of Virginia* (1624), which contained his last and most elaborate version of the Pocahontas story, as well as descriptions of Algonguian culture, politics, and religion.

1. Thomas Hariot

i. *A Briefe and True Report of the New Found Land of Virginia*
25-27

Some religion they haue alreadie, which although it be farre from the truth, yet beyng at [sic] it is, there is hope it may bee the easier and sooner reformed.

They beleeue that there are many Gods which they call *Mantóac*, but of different sortes and degrees; one onely chiefe and great God, which hath bene from all eternitie. Who as they affirme when hee purposed to make the worlde, made first other goddes of a principall order to bee as meanes and instruments to bee vsed in the creation and gouernment to follow; and after the Sunne, Moone, and Starres, as pettie goddes and the instruments of the other order more principall. First they say were made waters, out of which by the gods was made all diuersitie of creatures that are visible or inuisible.

For mankind they say a woman was made first, which by the woorking of one of the goddes, conceiued and brought foorth children: And in such sort they say they had their beginning.

But how manie yeeres or ages haue passed since, they say they can make no relation, hauing no letters nor other such meanes as we to keepe recordes of the particularities of times past, but onelie tradition from father to sonne.

They thinke that all the gods are of humane shape, & therfore they represent them by images in the formes of men, which they call *Kewasowok* one alone is called *Kewás*; Them they place in houses appropriate or temples which they call *Mathicómuck*; Where they woorship, praie, sing, and make manie times offerings vnto them. In some *Machicómuck* we haue seene but on[e] *Kewas*, in some two, and in other some three; The common sort thinke them to be also gods.

And this is the summe of their religion, which I learned by hauing special familiarity with some of their priestes. Wherein they were not so sure grounded, nor gaue such credite to their traditions and stories but through conuersing with vs they were brought into great doubts of their owne, and no small admiratiõ[1] of ours, with earnest desire in many, to learne more than we had meanes for want of perfect vtterance in their language to expresse.

Most things they sawe with vs, as Mathematicall instruments, sea compasses, the vertue of the loadstone in drawing yron, a perspectiue glasse whereby was shewed manie strange sightes, burning glasses, wildefire woorkes, gunnes, bookes, writing and reading, spring clocks that seeme to goe of themselues, and manie other thinges that wee had, were so straunge vnto them, and so farre exceeded their capacities to comprehend the reason and meanes how they should be made and done, that they thought they were rather the works of gods then of men, or at the leastwise they had bin giuen and taught vs of the gods. Which made manie of them to haue such opinion of vs, as that if they knew not the trueth of god and religion already, it was rather to be had from vs, whom God so specially loued then from a people that were so simple, as they found themselues to be in comparison of vs. Whereupon greater credite was giuen vnto that we spake of concerning such matters.

Manie times and in euery towne where I came, according as I was able, I made declaration of the contentes of the Bible; that therein was set foorth the true and onelie GOD, and his mightie woorkes, that therein was contayned the true doctrine of salutation through Christ, with manie particularities of Miracles and chiefe poyntes of religion, as I was able then to vtter, and thought fitte for the time. And although I told them the booke materially & of itself was not of anie such vertue, as I thought they did conceiue, but onely the doctrine therein cõtained; yet would many be glad to touch it, to embrace it, to kisse it, to hold it to their brests and heades, and stroke ouer all their bodie with it; to shewe their hungrie desire of that knowledge which was spoken of.

---

1 Admiration.

ii. *A Briefe and True Report of the New Found Land of Virginia*, illustrations by Theodore De Bry, 71–73

XXI.

Ther Idol Kiwasa.

The people of this cuntrie haue an Idol, which they call KIWASA: yt is carued of woode in lengthe 4. foote whose heade is like the heades of the people of Florida, the face is of a flesh colour, the brest white, the rest is all blacke, the thighes are also spottet with whitte. He hath a chayne abowt his necke of white beades, betweene which are other Rownde beades of copper which they esteeme more then golde or siluer. This Idol is placed in the temple of the towne of Secotam, as the keper of the kings dead corpses. Somtyme they haue two of thes idoles in theyr churches, and somtine 3. but never aboue, which they place in a darke corner wher they shew terrible. Thes poore soules haue none other knowledge of god although I thinke them verye Desirous to know the truthe. For when as wee kneeled downe on our knees to make our prayers vnto god, they went abowt to imitate vs, and when they saw we moued our lipps, they also dyd the like. Wherfore that is verye like that they might easelye be brongt to the knowledge of the gospel. God of his mercie grant them this grace.

XXII.

The Tombe of their Werowans or Cheiff Lordes.

The builde a Scaffolde 9. or 10. foote hihe as is expressed in this figure vnder the tõbs[1] of their Weroans, or cheefe lordes which they couer with matts, and lai the dead corpses of their weroans theruppon in manner followinge. First the bowells are taken forthe. Then layinge downe the skinne, they cutt all the flesh cleane from the bones, which the drye in the sonne, and

---

1   Tombs.

"Ther Idol Kiwasa," engraving by Theodor de Bry from Thomas Hariot, *A Briefe and True Report of the New Found Land of Virginia*, 1590. Courtesy of the Library of Congress.

well dryed the inclose in Matts, and place at their feete. Then their bones (remaininge still fastened together with the ligaments whole and vncorrupted) are couered a gayne with leather, and their carcase fashioned as yf their flesh wear not taken away. They lapp eache corps in his owne skinne after the same in thus handled, and lay yt in his order by the corpses of the other cheef lordes. By the dead bodies they sett their Idol Kiwasa, wher of we spake in the former chapiter: For they are persuaded that the same doth kepe the dead bodyes of their cheefe lordes that nothinge may hurt them. Moreouer vnder the foresaid scaffolde some on of their preists hath his lodginge, which Mumbleth his prayers nighte and day, and hath charge of the corpses. For his bedd he hath two deares skinnes spredd on the grownde, yf the wether bee cold hee maketh a fyre to warme by withall. Thes poore soules are thus instructed by nature to reuerence their princes euen after their death.

The trwe picture of a women

Picte II.

The woemen of the pictes aboue said wear noe worser for the
warres then the men. And wear paynted after the manner followinge, hauinge their heads bear, did lett their hairre flyinge.
abowt their Showlders wear painted with griffon heades, the
lowe parts and thighes with lion faces, or some other beaste as
yt commeth best into their fansye, their brest hath a maner of a
half moone, with a great stare, and fowre lesser in booth the
sides, their pappes painted in maner of beames of the sonne,
and amõg[1] all this a great litteninge starre vppon their brests.
The saids of som pointes or beames, and the hoolle bellye as a
sonne, the armes, thighes, and leggs well painted, of diuerses
Figures: The dyd also carye abowt theyr necks an ayern Ringe,
as the men did, and suche a girdle with the soorde hainginge,
hauinge a Picke or a lance in one hande, and twoe dardz in the
other.

2. George Percy, "Percy's Discourse of Virginia" 416-19

Captain Newport being gone for England, leaving us (one
hundred and foure persons) verie bare and scantie of victuals,
furthermore in warres and in danger of the Savages. We hoped
after a supply which Captaine Newport promised within twen-
tie weekes. But if the beginners of this action doe carefully further us, the Country being so fruitfull, it would be as great a
profit to the Realme of England, as the Indies to the King of
Spaine, if this River which wee have found had beene discovered in the time of warre with Spaine, it would have been a
commoditie to our Realme, and a great annoyance to our ene-
mies. The seven and twentieth of July the King of Rapahanna,

---

1 Among.

demanded a Canoa which was restored, lifted up his hand to the Sunne, which they worship as their God, besides he laid his hand on his heart, that he would be our speciall friend. It is a generall rule of these people when they swere by their God which is the Sunne, no Christian will keepe their Oath better upon this promise. These people have a great reverence to the Sunne above all other things at the rising and setting of the same, they sit downe lifting up their hands and eyes to the Sunne making a round Circle on the ground with dried Tobacco, then they began to pray making many Devillish gestures with a Hellish noise foming at the mouth, staring with their eyes, wagging their heads and hands in such a fashion and deformitie as it was monstrous to behold.

The sixt of August their died John Asbie of the bloudie Fluxe. The ninth day died George Flowre of the swelling. The tenth day died William Bruster Gentleman, of a wound given by the Savages, and was buried the eleventh day.

The fourteenth day, Jerome Alikock Ancient, died of a wound, the same day Francis Midwinter, Edward Moris Corporall died suddenly.

The fifteenth day, there died Edward Browne and Stephen Galthrope. The sixteenth day, there died Thomas Gower Gentleman. The seventeenth day, there died Thomas Mounslic. The eighteenth day, there died Robert Pennington, and John Martine Gentleman. The nineteenth day, died Dure Piggase Gentleman. The two and twentieth day of August, there died Captaine Bartholomew Gosnold one of our Councell, he was honourably buried, having all the Ordnance in the Fort shot off with many vollies of small shot.

After Captaine Gosnol's death, the Councell could hardly agree by the dissension of Captaine Kendall, which afterward was committed about hainous matters which was proved against him.

The foure and twentieth day, died Edward Harington and George Walker, and were buried the same day. The sixe and twentieth day, died Kenelme Throgmortine. The seven and twentieth day died William Roods. The eight and twentieth day died Thomas Stoodie, Cape Merchant.

The fourth day of September died Thomas Jacob Sergeant. The fift day, there died Benjamin Beast. Our men were destroyed with cruell diseases as Swellings, Fluxes, Burning Fevers, and by warres, and some departed suddenly, but for the most part they died of meere famine. There were never Englishmen left in a forreigne Countrey in such miserie as wee were in this new discovered Virginia. Wee watched every three nights lying on the bare cold ground what weather soever came warded all the next day, which brought our men to bee most feeble wretches, our food was but a small Can of Barlie sod in water to five men a day, our drinke cold water taken out of the River, which was at a floud verie salt, at a low tide full of slime and filth, which was the destruction of many of our men. Thus we lived for the space of five moneths in this miserable distresse, not having five able men to man our Bulwarkes upon any occasion. If it had not pleased God to have put a terrour in the Savages' hearts, we had all perished by those vild and cruell Pagans, being in that weake estate as we were; our men night and day groaning in every corner of the Fort most pittifull to heare, if there were any conscience in men, it would make their harts to bleed to heare the pittiful murmurings & out-cries of our sick men without reliefe every night and day for the space of sixe weekes, some departing out of the World, many times three or foure in a night, in the morning their bodies trailed out of their Cabines like Dogges to be buried: in this sort did I see the mortalitie of divers of our people.

It pleased God, after a while, to send those people which were our mortall enemies to releeve us with victuals, as Bread, Corne, Fish, and Flesh in great plentie, which was the setting up of our feeble men, otherwise wee had all perished. Also we were frequented by divers Kings in the Countrie, bringing us store of provision to our great comfort.

The eleventh day, there was certaine Articles laid against Master Wingfield which was then President, thereupon he was not only displaced out of his President ship, but was also from being of the Councell. Afterwards Captain John Ratcliffe was chosen President.

The eighteenth day, died one Ellis Kinistone which was starved to death with cold. The same day at night, died one Richard Simmons. The nineteenth day, there died one Thomas Mouton.

William White (having lived with the Natives) reported to us of their customes in the morning by breake of day, before they eate or drinke both men, women and children, that be above tenne yeeres of age runnes into the water, there washes themselves a good while till the Sun riseth, then offer Sacrifice to it, strewing Tobacco on the water or land, honouring the Sunne as their God, likewise they doe at the setting of the Sunne.

3. John Smith

i. *The Generall Historie of Virginia* 64-65

The next day came divers Boats, and in one of them the Kings Brother, with forty or fifty men, proper people, and in their behaviour very civill; his name was Granganamco, the King is called Wingina, the Country Wingandacoa. Leaving his Boats a little from our Ships, he came with his trayne to the poynt: where spreading a Matte he sat downe. Though we came to him well armed, he made signes to us to sit downe without any shew of feare, stroking his head and brest, and also ours, to expresse his love. After he had made a long speech unto us, we presented him with divers toyes, which he kindly accepted. He was greatly regarded by his people, for none of them did sit, nor speake a word, but foure, on whom we bestowed presents also, but he tooke all from them, making signes all things did belong to him....

... my selfe with seaven more went twenty myle into the River Occam, that runneth toward the Cittie Skicoack, and the evening following we came to an Ile called Roanoak, from the harbour where we entred 7. leagues; at the North end was 9. houses, builded with Cedar, fortified round with sharpe trees, and the entrance like a Turnpik. When we came towards it, the wife of Granganameo came running out to meete us, (her husband was absent) commanding her people to draw our Boat ashore for beating on the billowes, other she appoynted to carry us on their backes aland, others to bring our Ores into the house for[1] stealing. When we came into the other roome, (for there was five in the house) she caused us to sit downe by a great fire; after tooke off our clothes and washed them, of some our stockings, and some our feete in warme water, and she her selfe tooke much paines to see all things well ordered, and to provide us victuall....

... This discovery was so welcome into England that it pleased her Majestie to call this Country of Wingandacoa, Virginia, by which name now you are to understand how it was planted, disolved, renued, and enlarged....

ii. *The Generall Historie of Virginia* 121-22; 125

There is yet in Virginia no place discovered to be so Savage, in which they have not a Religion, Deere, and Bow, and Arrowes. All things that are able to doe them hurt beyond their prevention, they adore with their kinde of divine worship; as the fire, water, lightning, thunder, our Ordnance, peeces, horses, etc. But their chiefe God they worship is the Devill. Him they call *Okee*, and serve him more of feare then love. They say they have conference with him, and fashion themselves as neare to his shape as they can imagine. In their Temples they have his image evill favouredly carved, and then painted and adorned with chaines of copper, and beads, and covered with a skin, in such manner as the deformitie may well suit with such a God. By him is commonly the sepulcher of their Kings. Their bodies are first bowelled, then dried upon hurdles till they be very dry, and so about the most of their joynts and necke they hang bracelets, or chaines of copper, pearle, and such like, as they use to weare, their inwards they stuffe with copper beads, hatchets, and such trash. Then lappe they them very carefully in white skins, and so rowle them in mats for their winding sheets. And

---

1   In his edition of Smith, Barbour inserts [fear of] here (66).

in the Tombe which is an arch made of mats, they lay them orderly. What remaineth of this kinde of wealth their Kings have, they set at their feet in baskets. These Temples and bodies are kept by their Priests....

In every Territory of a Werowance is a Temple and a Priest, two or three or more. Their principall Temple or place of superstition is at Uttamussack at Pamaunkee, neare unto which is a house, Temple, or place of Powhatans.

Upon the top of certaine red sandy hils in the woods, there are three great houses filled with images of their Kings, and Devils, and Tombes of their Predecessors. Those houses are neare sixtie foot in length built arbour-wise, after their building. This place they count so holy as that but the Priests and Kings dare come into them; nor the Salvages dare not goe up the river in boats by it, but they solemnly cast some peece of copper, white beads, or *Pocones* into the river, for feare their *Okee* should be offended and revenged of them.

Thus,

> *Feare was the first their Gods begot:*
> *Till feare began, their Gods were not.*

They thinke that their Werowances and Priests which they also esteeme *Quiyoughcosughes*, when they are dead, doe goe beyond the mountaines towards the setting of the sunne, and ever remaine there in forme of their *Okee*, with their heads painted with oyle and *Pocones*, finely trimmed with feathers, and shall have beads, hatchets, copper, and Tobacco, doing nothing but dance and sing, with all their Predecessors. But the common people they suppose shall not live after death, but rot in their graves like dead dogs.

To divert them from this blind Idolatry, we did our best endevours, chiefly with the Werowance of Quiyoughcoha-nock, whose devotion, apprehension, and good disposition, much exceeded any in those Countries, who although we could not as yet prevaile, to forsake his false Gods, yet this he did beleeve that our God as much exceeded theirs, as our Gunnes did their Bowes and Arrowes, and many times did send to me to James Towne, intreating me to pray to my God for raine, for their Gods would not send them any. And in this lamentable ignorance doe these poore soules sacrifice themselves to the Devill, not knowing their Creator; and we had not language sufficient, so plainly to expresse it as make them understand it; which God grant they may.

For,

> *Religion 'tis that doth distinguish us,*
> *From their bruit humor, well we may it know;*
> *That can with understanding argue thus,*
> *Our God is truth, but they cannot doe so.*

iii. *The Generall Historie of Virginia* 150-52; 198-99; 245-46; 251; 258; 261-62; 294-95

At last they brought him[1] to Meronocomoco, where was Powhatan their Emperor. Here more then two hundred of those grim Courtiers stood wondering at him, as he had beene a monster; till Powhatan and his trayne had put themselves in their greatest braveries. Before a fire upon a seat like a bedsted, he sat covered with a great robe, made of Rarowcun skinnes, and all the tayles hanging by. On either hand did sit a young wench of 16 or 18 yeares, and along on each side the house, two rowes of men, and behind them as many women, with all their heads and shoulders painted red; many of their heads bedecked with the white downe of Birds; but every one with something: and a great chayne of white beads about their necks. At his entrance before the King, all the people gave a great shout. The Queene of Appamatuck was appointed to bring him water to wash his hands, and another brought him a bunch of feathers, in stead of a Towell to dry them: having feasted him after their best barbarous manner they could, a long consultation was held, but the conclusion was, two great stones were brought before Powhatan: then as many as could layd hands on him, dragged him to them, and thereon laid his head, and being ready with their clubs, to beate out his braines, Poca-

---

1 Smith, taken captive.

hontas the Kings dearest daughter, when no intreaty could prevaile, got his head in her armes, and laid her owne upon his to save him from death: whereat the Emperour was contented he should live to make him hatchets, and her bells, beads, and copper; for they thought him as well of all occupations as themselves. For the King himselfe will make his owne robes, shooes, bowes, arrowes, pots; plant, hunt, or doe any thing so well as the rest....

Two dayes after, Powhatan having disguised himselfe in the most fearefullest manner he could, caused Captaine Smith to be brought forth to a great house in the woods, and there upon a mat by the fire to be left alone. Not long after from behinde a mat that divided the house, was made the most dolefullest noyse he ever heard; then Powhatan more like a devill then a man with some two hundred more as blacke as himselfe, came unto him and told him now they were friends, and presently he should goe to James towne, to send him two great gunnes, and a gryndstone, for which he would give him the Country of Capahowosick, and for ever esteeme him as his soone Nantaquoud. So to James towne with 12 guides Powhatan sent him. That night they quarterd in the woods, he still expecting (as he had done all this long time of his imprisonment) every houre to be put to one death or other: for all their feasting. But almightie God (by his divine providence) had mollified the hearts of those sterne Barbarians with compassion....

... Powhatan and his Dutch-men brusting with desire to have the head of Captaine Smith, for if they could but kill him, they thought all was theirs, neglected not any opportunity to effect his purpose. The Indians with all the merry sports they could devise, spent the time till night: then they all returned to Powhatan, who all this time was making ready his forces to surprise the house and him at supper. Notwithstanding the eternall all-seeing God did prevent him, and by a strange meanes. For Pocahontas his dearest jewell and daughter, in that darke night came through the irksome woods, and told our Captaine great cheare should be sent us by and by: but Powhatan and all the power he could make, would after come kill us all, if they that brought it could not kill us with our owne weapons when we were at supper. Therefore if we would live shee wished us presently to bee gone. Such things as shee delighted in, he would have given her: but with the teares running downe her cheekes, shee said shee durst not be seene to have any: for if Powhatan should know it, she were but dead, and so shee ranne away by her selfe as she came....

Long before this, Master John Rolfe, an honest Gentleman, and of good behaviour, had beene in love with Pocahontas, and she with him, which thing at that instant I made knowne to Sir Thomas Dale by a letter from him, wherein hee intreated his advice, and she acquainted her brother with it, which resolution Sir Thomas Dale well approved: the brute of this mariage came soone to the knowledge of Powhatan, a thing acceptable to him, as appeared by his sudden consent, for within ten daies he sent Opachisco, an old Uncle of hers, and two of his sons, to see the manner of the mariage, and to doe in that behalfe what they were requested, for the confirmation thereof, as his deputie; which was accordingly done about the first of Aprill: And ever since wee have had friendly trade and commerce, as well with Powhatan himself, as all his subjects....

I have read the substance of this relation, in a Letter written by Sir Thomas Dale, another by Master Whitaker, and a third by Master John Rolfe; how carefull they were to instruct her in Christianity, and how capable and desirous shee was thereof, after she had beene some time thus tutored, shee never had desire to goe to her father, nor could well endure the society of her owne nation: the true affection she constantly bare her husband was much, and the strange apparitions and violent passions he endured for her love, as he deeply protested, was wonderful, and she openly renounced her countries idolatry, confessed the faith of Christ, and was baptized, but either the coldnesse of the adventurers, or the bad usage of that was collected, or both, caused this worthy Knight to write thus....

During this time, the Lady Rebecca, alias Pocahontas, daughter to Powhatan, by the diligent care of Master John Rolfe her husband and her friends, was taught to speake such English as might well bee understood, well instructed in Christianitie, and was become very formall and civill after our English manner; shee had also by him a childe which she loved most dearely, and the Treasurer and Company tooke order both for the maintenance of her and it, besides there were divers persons of great ranke and qualitie had beene very kinde to her; and before she arrived at London, Captaine Smith to deserve her former courtesies, made her qualities knowne to the Queenes most excellent Majestie and her Court, and writ a little booke to this effect to the Queene: ...

The small time I staid in London, divers Courtiers and others, my acquaintances, hath gone with mee to see her, that generally concluded, they did thinke God had a great hand in her conversion, and they have seene many English Ladies worse favoured, proportioned and behavioured, and as since I have heard, it pleased both the King and Queenes Majestie honourably to esteeme her, accompanied with that honourable Lady the Lady De la Ware, and that honourable Lord her husband, and divers other persons of good qualities, both publikely at the maskes and otherwise, to her great satisfaction and content, which doubtlesse she would have deserved, had she lived to arrive in Virginia....

The Treasurer, Councell and Companie, having well furnished Captaine Samuel Argall, the Lady Pocahontas alias Rebecca, with her husband and others, in the good ship called the *George*, it pleased God at Gravesend to take this young Lady to his mercie, where shee made not more sorrow for her unexpected death, than joy to the beholders, to heare and see her make so religious and godly an end. Her little childe Thomas Rolfe therefore was left at Plimoth with Sir Lewis Stukly, that desire the keeping of it....

Having occasion to send to Opechankanough about the middle of March, hee used the Messenger well, and told him he held the peace so firme, the sky should fall or he dissolved it; yet such was the treachery of those people, when they had contrived our destruction, even but two daies before the massacre, they guided our men with much kindnesse thorow the woods, and one Browne that lived among them to learne the language, they sent home to his Master; yea, they borrowed our Boats to transport themselves over the River, to consult on the devilish murder that issued, and of our utter extirpation, which God of his mercy (by the meanes of one of themselves converted to Christianitie) prevented, and as well on the Friday morning that fatall day, being the two and twentieth of March, as also in the evening before, as at other times they came unarmed into our houses, with Deere, Turkies, Fish, Fruits, and other provisions to sell us, yea in some places sat downe at breakfast with our people, whom immediately with their owne tooles they slew most barbarously, not sparing either age or sex, man woman or childe, so sudden in their execution, that few or none discerned the weapon or blow that brought them to destruction: In which manner also they slew many of our people at severall works in the fields, well knowing in what places and quarters each of our men were, in regard of their familiaritie with us, for the effecting that great master-peece of worke their conversion; and by this meanes fell that fatall morning under the bloudy and barbarous hands of that perfidious and inhumane people, three hundred forty seven men, women and children, most by thier owne weapons, and not being content with their lives, they fell againe upon the dead bodies, making as well as they could a fresh murder, defacing, dragging, and mangling their dead carkases into many peeces, and carying some parts away in derision, with base and brutish triumph....

That worthy religious Gentleman Master George Thorp, Deputie to the College lands, sometimes one of his Majesties Pensioners, and in command one of the principall in Virginia; did so truly affect their conversion, that whosoever under him did them the least displeasure, were punished severely. He thought nothing too deare for them, he never denied them any thing, in so much that when they complained that our Mastives did feare them, he to content them in all things, caused some of them to be killed in their presence, to the great displeasure of the owners, and would have had all the rest guelt to make them the milder, might he have had his will. The King dwelling but in a Cottage, he built him a faire house after the English fashion, in which he tooke such pleasure, especially in the locke and key, which he so admired, as locking and unlocking his doore a hundred times a day, he thought no device in the world comparable to it.

Thus insinuating himselfe into this Kings favour for his religious purpose, he conferred oft with him about Religion, as many other in this former Discourse had done, and this Pagan confessed to him as he did to them, our God was better then theirs, and seemed to be much pleased with that Discourse, and of his company, and to requite all those courtesies; yet this viperous brood did, as the sequell shewed, not onely murder him, but with such spight and scorne abused his dead corps as is unfitting to be heard with civill eares....

Appendix C: Reviews of The Female American

Only two brief notices of *The Female American* appeared when the novel was first published in 1767, both in English journals devoted to literary reviews. There are no extant reviews of either the 1800 or 1814 editions, and apparently no reviews of any of the three editions of the novel appeared in America.

1. *The Monthly Review; or, Literary Journal* vol. 36 (1767) 238.

A sort of second *Robinson Crusoe*; full of wonders; and well calculated to make one sort of readers *stare*.

2. *The Critical Review; or, Annals of Literature* vol. 23 (1767) 217.

Mrs. Unca Eliza Winkfield is a most strange adventurer, and her memoirs seem to be calculated only for the wild Indians to whom she is so closely allied. We could therefore have wished, as well for her sake as our own, that this lady had published her adventures at the Fall of Niagara, or upon the Banks of Lake Superior, as she would then, probably, have received the most judicious and sincere applause from her enlightened countrymen and princely relations, and have saved us six hours very disagreeable employment.

Works Cited/Recommended Reading

Aland, Barbara, et. al. *The Greek New Testament*. Stuttgart: Deutsche Bibelgesellschaft, 1993.

Armstrong, Nancy and Leonard Tennenhouse. *The Imaginary Puritan: Literature, Intellectual Labor, and the Origins of Personal Life*. Berkeley: U of California P, 1992.

Aubin, Penelope. *The Life of Charlotta Du Pont*. London, 1723.

Baine, Rodney M. *Daniel Defoe and the Supernatural*. Athens: U of Georgia P, 1968.

Behn, Aphra. *Oroonoko*. 1688. New York: Norton, 1973.

Blackwell, Jeannine. "An Island of Her Own: Heroines of the German Robinsonades from 1720 to 1800." *The German Quarterly* (1985): 5-26.

Brophy, Elizabeth Bergen. *Women's Lives and the 18th-Century Novel*. Tampa: U of South Florida P, 1991.

Brown, Laura. *Ends of Empire: Women and Ideology in Early Eighteenth-Century English Literature*. Ithaca: Cornell UP, 1993.

Burnham, Michelle. *Captivity and Sentiment: Cultural Exchange in American Literature, 1682-1861*. Hanover: UP of New England, 1997.

Castiglia, Christopher. *Bound and Determined: Captivity, Culture-Crossing, and White Womanhood from Mary Rowlandson to Patty Hearst*. Chicago: U of Chicago P, 1996.

A Collection of Papers, Printed by Order of the Society for the Propagation of the Gospel in Foreign Parts. London, 1706.

The Critical Review; or, Annals of Literature. By A Society of Gentlemen. Vol. 23. London, 1767.

Cross, Arthur Lyon. *The Anglican Episcopate and the American Colonies*. Hamden, Conn.: Archon Books, 1964.

Defoe, Daniel. *Robinson Crusoe*. 1719. Ed. J. Donald Crowley. Oxford: Oxford UP, 1972.

——. *Serious Reflections During the Life and Surprising Adventures of Robinson Crusoe*. 1720. New York: Thomas Crowell & Co., 1903.

Demos, John. *The Unredeemed Captive*. New York: Knopf, 1994.

Dharwadker, Aparna. "Nation, Race, and the Ideology of Commerce in Defoe." *The Eighteenth Century* 39 (1998): 63–84.

Dibdin, Charles. *Hannah Hewit; or, the Female Crusoe.* London, 1792.

Dugaw, Diane. *Warrior Women and Popular Balladry 1650-1850.* Cambridge: Cambridge UP, 1989.

Eliot, John. *A Late and Further Manifestation of the Progress of the Gospel amongst the Indians in New-England.* London, 1655.

——. *John Eliot's Indian Dialogues: A Study in Cultural Interaction.* Ed. Henry W. Bowden and James P. Ronda. Westport, Conn.: Greenwood Press, 1980.

Green, Martin. *The Robinson Crusoe Story.* University Park: Pennsylvania State UP, 1990.

Hariot, Thomas. *A Briefe and True Report of the New Found Land of Virginia.* 1590. New York: Dover, 1972.

Heilman, Robert Bechtold. *America in English Fiction 1760-1800.* 1937. Repr. New York: Octagon Books, 1968.

Hulme, Peter. *Colonial Encounters: Europe and the Native Caribbean 1492-1797.* London: Routledge, 1986.

Hunter, J. Paul. *The Reluctant Pilgrim: Defoe's Emblematic Method and Quest for Form in* Robinson Crusoe. Baltimore: Johns Hopkins UP, 1966.

Kolodny, Annette. *The Land Before Her: Fantasy and Experience of the American Frontiers 1630-1860.* Chapel Hill: U of North Carolina P, 1984.

Lennox, Charlotte. *The Life of Harriot Stuart.* 1751. Madison: Fairleigh Dickinson UP, 1995.

Lesage, Alain-René. *Aventures du Chevalier de Beauchêne.* 1732. Paris: Impr. De LeBlanc, 1910.

Longueville, Peter. *The Hermit.* 1727. New York: Garland Publishing, 1972.

McDowell, Tremaine. "An American Robinson Crusoe." *American Literature* 1 (1929-30): 307-09.

McKeon, Michael. *The Origins of the English Novel 1600-1740.* Baltimore: Johns Hopkins UP, 1987.

The Monthly Review; or, Literary Journal. Vol. 36. London, 1767.

Marouby, Christian. "Utopian Colonialism." *North Dakota Quarterly* 56.3 (1988): 148-60.

"No More Separate Spheres!" Special issue ed. by Cathy N. Davidson. *American Literature* 70.3 (1998).

Percy, George. "Percy's Discourse of Virginia." 1606. *Hakluytus Posthumus or Purchas His Pilgrimes.* By Samuel Purchas. 1625. Vol. 18. Glasgow: James MacLehose and Sons, 1905. 403-19.

Rogers, Robert. *Ponteach; Or the Savages of America.* 1766. New York: B. Franklin, 1971.

Rowlandson, Mary. *The Sovereignty and Goodness of God.* 1682. Ed. Neal Salisbury. Boston: Bedford Books, 1997.

Rowson, Susanna. *Reuben and Rachel; or, Tales of Old Times.* Boston, 1798.

Seaver, James. *A Narrative of the Life of Mrs. Mary Jemison.* 1824. Ed. June Namias. Norman: U of Oklahoma P, 1992.

Slotkin, Richard. *Regeneration Through Violence: The Mythology of the American Frontier, 1600-1860.* Middletown, Conn.: Wesleyan UP, 1973.

Smith, John. *Generall History of Virginia.* 1624. In *The Complete Works of Captain John Smith.* Vol. II. Ed. Philip Barbour. Chapel Hill: U of North Carolina P, 1986. 3-475.

Smith, William. *An Historical Account of the Expedition Against the Ohio Indians.* Philadelphia, 1765.

Spengemann, William C. *A Mirror for Americanists: Reflections on the Idea of American Literature.* Hanover: UP of New England, 1989.

Waterhouse, Edward. *A Declaration of the State of the Colony in Virginia.* 1622. New York: Da Capo Press, 1970.

Watt, Ian. *The Rise of the Novel: Studies in Defoe, Richardson, and Fielding.* Berkeley: U of California P, 1957.

White, Michael. "Reading and Rewriting: The Production of an Economic *Robinson Crusoe.*" *Southern Review* 15.2 (1982): 115-42.

[Wilson, Thomas.] *An Essay Towards an Instruction For the Indians.* London: 1740.

Wingfield, Edward Maria. "A Discourse on Virginia." In *The Jamestown Voyages Under the First Charter 1606-1609.* Vol. I. Ed. Philip Barbour. Cambridge: Hakluyt Society at Cambridge UP, 1969. 213-34.

Wingfield, Jocelyn R. *Virginia's True Founder: Edward-Maria Wingfield and His Times 1550-c.1614.* Athens GA: The Wingfield Family Society, 1993.